FROM PEARL HARBOR
TO SAIGON

THE HAYMARKET SERIES

Editors: Mike Davis and Michael Sprinker

The Haymarket Series offers original studies in politics, history and culture with a focus on North America. Representing views across the American left on a wide range of subjects, the series will be of interest to socialists both in the USA and throughout the world. A century after the first May Day, the American left remains in the shadow of those martyrs whom the Haymarket Series honors and commemorates. These studies testify to the living legacy of political activism and commitment for which they gave their lives.

RECENT AND FORTHCOMING TITLES

The Invention of the White Race, Volume 2: The Origin of Racial Oppression in Anglo-America by Theodore Allen

Pickup Artists: Street Basketball in America by Lars Anderson and Chad Millman

Cultures in Babylon: Black Britain and African America by Hazel V. Carby

Glitter, Stucco and Dumpster Diving: Reflections on Building Production in the Vernacular City by John Chase

Prisoners of the American Dream: Politics and Economy in the History of the US Working Class (new edition) by Mike Davis

Mechanic Accents: Dime Novels and Working-Class Culture in America (new edition) and *The Cultural Front: The Laboring of American Culture in the Twentieth Century* by Michael Denning

The Sixties Chicano Movement: Youth, Identity, Power (new edition) by Carlos Muñoz

Red Dirt: Growing Up Okie by Roxanne Dunbar Ortiz

Structures of the Jazz Age: Mass Culture, Progressive Education and Racial Discourse in American Modernist Fiction by Chip Rhodes

The Wages of Whiteness: Race and the Making of the American Working Class (new edition) by David R. Roediger

A Plague on Your Houses: How New York was Burned Down and National Public Health Crumbled by Deborah Wallace and Rodrick Wallace

Development Arrested: The Blues and Plantation Power in the Mississippi Delta by Clyde Woods

FROM PEARL HARBOR TO SAIGON

Japanese American Soldiers
and the Vietnam War

TOSHIO WHELCHEL

VERSO
London • New York

First published by Verso 1999
© Toshio Whelchel 1999
All rights reserved

Verso
UK: 6 Meard Street, London W1V 3HR
US: 180 Varick Street, New York, NY 10014–4606

Verso is the imprint of New Left Books

ISBN 1–85984–859–1

British Library Cataloguing in Publication Data
A catalogue record for this book is available from the British Library

Library of Congress Cataloging-in-Publication Data
Whelchel, Toshio,
    From Pearl Harbor to Saigon : Japanese American soldiers and the
Vietnam War / Toshio Whelchel.
        p.   cm.
    Includes bibliographical references.
    ISBN 1–85984–859–1 (cloth)
    1. Vietnamese Conflict. 1961–1975—Participation. Japanese
American.   2. Vietnamese Conflict. 1961–1975—Japanese Americans
Interviews.   3. Japanese American veterans—California Interviews.
I. Title.
DS559.8.J35W47   1999
959.704'3352—dc21   99–24367
                                                              CIP

Typeset by SetSystems Ltd, Saffron Walden, Essex
Printed by Biddles Ltd, Guildford and King's Lynn

To the memories of

my father
Wayne Edward Whelchel (1918–1965)

father-in-law
William Z. Landworth (1925–1986)

and maternal uncle
Mori Yoshihiro (1920–1990)

CONTENTS

CONTENTS

CONTENTS

LIST OF ILLUSTRATIONS

MAPS

PHOTOGRAPHS

Photographs appear between pages 106 and 107.

PREFACE

Among Vietnam veterans, Japanese Americans have remained silent about their own wartime experiences until quite recently. In many instances their silence reflected their parents' reluctance to recall World War II internment camp experiences—experiences which too often left victims bewildered and resentful, and which for many led to a poorer quality of life after release. Yet this silence also reflected a wish, and sometimes a need, to suppress recollection of a period of the veterans' lives during which they faced questions not only about their role in a brutally "modern" war, but also about their identity as Japanese Americans fighting for the US military on Asian territory.

My initial motivation for this project came through reading Christian Appy's seminal book, *Working-Class War* (1993): I wanted to explore how the limited choices of people with working-class backgrounds affected them as they faced the Vietnam War draft. But this desire was quickly stymied by my lack of contacts.

I began by contacting VFW (Veterans of Foreign Wars) posts and local veteran counseling centers throughout the greater Los Angeles area, making inquiries about Japanese American Vietnam veterans who might be members or attendees, all without any success. I attended a local Veterans' Day Parade with the hope of meeting Japanese American Vietnam vets but, to my dismay, not a single Asian vet marched with the Vietnam veterans' contingent—though there was a large group of old Japanese American veterans from World War II. I did speak with other

Vietnam veterans who marched in the parade and with vets watching from the sidewalk, all without gaining any significant contacts. In fact, the white Vietnam veterans I spoke with after the parade were quite hostile and belligerent when I made initial inquiries concerning their time spent in Vietnam: perhaps my "Asian" face triggered a negative reaction. At one point, a retired Samoan Marine Corps gunnery sergeant intervened to maintain civility between the incensed and irate veterans and me.

Finally, after contacting a staff member of a local Japanese American newspaper, I was advised to approach a highly decorated Japanese American combat vet living in Los Angeles. Through his contacts I was able to break into a core group of local veterans, who in turn provided additional contacts through personal introductions and friends.

During 1995, I contacted approximately one hundred Asian American and non-Asian American Vietnam veterans from around the Los Angeles area, as well as from San Diego, San Jose, and San Francisco, and spoke with vets from around the nation. Out of this initial contact group I interviewed fifty-nine Asian American veterans.

For many of these men, our one-on-one dialogue was their first real exchange about their Vietnam experiences: a significant number had concealed this pivotal period of their lives from their parents, friends, wives, and children. Around a tenth of those originally contacted wouldn't even discuss Vietnam and were adamant in their refusal to be interviewed. Those who were willing to meet with me were at times reluctant either to engage their memories themselves or to disclose what was being recalled. In the course of an interview many tried to evade the traumatic and tragic memories of losing fellow soldiers, of firefights, and the sheer terror of combat, and my attempts to encourage detailed descriptions of events were at times completely rebuffed. For example, a former helicopter crew chief told me reluctantly that, yes, he did participate in the random shooting of civilians from the helicopters, but then refused to say anything more. A small number of vets initially showed interest in

discussing their Vietnam experiences, but once they found out that the interviews would probe their combat experiences they either changed their minds about giving the interview or simply did not show up at our designated meeting place. I contacted one veteran in San Jose who invited me to his restaurant for the interview. I flew to the city, rented a car, and drove to meet him, but he did not show up. I met him later in the evening, but he was unwilling to discuss his combat experiences.

Consequently, the interviews I finally gathered were often the result of an emotional outburst of memories intermingled with intense feelings of outrage, anxiety, and exhilaration, and softened by solemn reflections on a war which for them ended close to thirty years ago. The tears shed by the vets as they recalled the loss of comrades and friends were infectious. Having drinks together during the interview became a not uncommon ritual. I enjoyed the long hours spent over bottles of beer, shots of whiskey and scotch, and, on one occasion, an exquisite platter of sashimi and hot sake as the interview progressed.

The eleven interviews selected and published here represent a diverse range of wartime experience. Three of the eleven veterans were former Marines who either volunteered to avoid the draft or were forced to enlist as a consequence of court orders, and eight were Army draftees and enlistees. Demographically, the veterans represent a cross-section of Japanese Americans from various parts of greater Los Angeles, such as East Los Angeles, Crenshaw, South Central, San Fernando Valley, and Gardena. Their narratives are presented chronologically, beginning with a veteran who was in Vietnam from 1965, when the first Marine Corps units arrived in Danang, and ending with a soldier who was there in 1971, when the war was close to its end. The veterans' wartime locations also cover a comprehensive geographical range: non-combatant Army administrators stationed in Saigon, Nha Trang, or Camp Enari; an Army conscientious

objector working as a medic along the Mekong River; Marines stationed along the Demilitarized Zone, in isolated villages, as part of a Marine Corps pacification program; Marines stationed on a hilltop outside of Danang—experiences which span the entire length of South Vietnam.

Thematically, the interviews were conducted around four key areas of concern: first, the veterans' pre-war experiences of growing up in southern California, where the likely limitation in life choices led many working-class Japanese American youths to be vulnerable to the military draft; second, their experience of basic training, determined by whether they chose to enlist in the Marine Corps or the Army, and the ensuing conflicts for Asian youths fighting for US military institutions engaged in an essentially Asian war; third, their selection of military jobs and the resulting experience in Vietnam; and fourth, their experiences upon returning home and the various decisions they made subsequently. These four strands also form the structure of the introduction, which attempts to provide something of an overview of the Japanese American veteran's experience of Vietnam. To this end, it includes quotations not just from the eleven key interviewees, but also from some of the other veterans I spoke with.

Throughout, I have used pseudonyms to protect the privacy and confidentiality of the veterans in these oral recollections. As requested by many of the vets, I have also restricted the use of personal information, as much as possible, to protect identities. The issue of confidentiality was paramount and, without the reassurance of personal anonymity in discussing their innermost feelings and reflections, most of the vets would not have permitted me an interview. For some, as I have suggested, the promise of confidentiality and the use of pseudonyms were still insufficient to bring them to reveal their stories.

T.W.
August 1998

GLOSSARY

Agent Orange
Toxic herbicide, 2, 4, 5-T (Dioxin), sprayed on vegetation throughout South Vietnam. Eleven million gallons sprayed over 5.7 million acres between 1965 and 1970.

AIT
Advanced Individual Training. Specialized military training school after basic training for enlisted personnel.

Algonquins
One of many Japanese American urban gangs dating from the fifties and sixties. Other urban gangs associated with the Japanese American community were the Black Juans, Gardena Boys, Ministers, Buddha Bandits, and Satan's Sinners.

ARVN
Army of the Republic of Vietnam; South Vietnamese regular troops.

Blue Dragons
Designation of 2nd Korean Marine Brigade in South Vietnam.

CAP
Combined Action Program. US Marine Corps' village-level counterinsurgency program to win the "hearts and minds" of the South Vietnamese.

CIA
Central Intelligence Agency. American intelligence involvement in Vietnam began in 1943, when OSS (Office of Strategic Services) agents

supported the Vietminh against the Japanese. CIA involvement in clandestine covert operations in Vietnam dated from the 1950s to the early 1970s.

CO

Conscientious Objector. Approximately 170,000 Americans received deferment from the draft as conscientious objectors during the Vietnam War. In addition, 600,000 evaded the draft and 30,000–50,000 fled to Canada.

I Corps

One of four military regions (I, II, III, IV Corps), comprising five northern provinces of South Vietnam controlled by US forces.

DI

Drill Instructor.

DMZ

Demilitarized Zone. The 17th parallel where South and North Vietnam were temporarily divided.

domino theory

Central tenet of US administrations from Eisenhower to Nixon, which held that Communist domination of Vietnam would lead inevitably to Communist control of all Southeast Asian nations.

Dow Chemical

US chemical corporation responsible for manufacturing 2, 4, 5-T (Dioxin)-
based herbicides (Agent Orange, White, and Blue) used in Vietnam.

Gidra

Radical Asian American newspaper published in Los Angeles between 1969 and 1974. Placed under FBI's counterintelligence surveillance.

gook

A derogatory term used by US troops in reference to Asians in general and to Vietnamese in particular during the Vietnam War. Other terms used were zips, slopes, and zipper-heads.

Ho Chi Minh

Founder of the Indochinese Communist Party in 1930. President of the Democratic Republic of Vietnam from 1945 until his death in 1969.

hooch

Military barracks or tent.

issei

First-generation emigrants from Japan who settled in the United States between 1898 and 1930.

kibei

Second-generation Japanese American (*nisei*) born in the US but educated in Japan.

Manzanar

One of ten internment camps run by the US military from 1942 to 1946, where Americans of Japanese ethnicity were imprisoned during World War II.

Robert McNamara

Secretary of Defense from 1961 to 1968; architect of the Vietnam War under the Johnson administration.

MCRD

Marine Corps Recruit Depot located in San Diego, California. One of two Marine Corps training depots in the country; the other is in Parris Island, South Carolina.

montagnards

Indigenous mountain people of Vietnam. The name is a French term meaning "mountain people." Montagnards were recruited by the US to support Special Forces (Green Berets) against the North.

MPC

Military Payment Certificate—paper currency issued in lieu of cash to soldiers in Vietnam.

nisei

Second-generation Japanese American born between 1918 and 1922.

The *nisei* generation came of legal age between 1939 and 1943, forming the majority of Japanese Americans who served in segregated Army units during World War II.

Pentagon Papers

Secret military documents written between 1967 and 1969, describing US involvement in Vietnam from 1945 to 1968. In 1971 they were leaked to the national media by Daniel Ellsberg.

Phoenix

CIA program headed by William Colby, using joint US and South Vietnamese troops to assassinate South Vietnamese revolutionaries while destroying their political and military infrastructure. From 1968 to 1972 approximately 26,000 suspected revolutionaries were killed.

PTSD

Post-Traumatic Stress Disorder. Combat-related stress disorder experienced by US war veterans upon returning from Vietnam.

RPG

Rocket-propelled grenade used by South Vietnamese revolutionaries and by North Vietnamese regular troops.

sansei

Third-generation Japanese Americans.

sappers

Vietnamese revolutionaries trained to infiltrate and attack US military bases using explosives and mines.

VC

Viet Cong; a derogatory term used by the US and South Vietnamese to refer to Vietnamese Communist revolutionaries.

Vietnam Veterans Against the War

One of many anti-war groups, composed of Vietnam War veterans and active in the early part of the seventies.

yonsei

Fourth-generation Japanese Americans.

FROM PEARL HARBOR
TO SAIGON

Friend, we must cling to what little
the war didn't take: our voices,
the singular vision, that hard sleep
from which you jump
as if you've seen something.
You have. And I have.[1]

Southeast Asian nations such as Malaysia, Indonesia, the Philippines, Laos, Cambodia, and Vietnam have been the sites of Western colonialism and imperialism since the mid-nineteenth century. The French—having secured Vietnam as their Asian colonial outpost in 1865—in particular waged colonial war against Vietnamese nationalists and revolutionaries from 1946 until 1954. During this time America's role in Vietnam was limited to providing financial and military support to the French through the Marshall Plan: its first military mission was sent in the postwar period, following President Truman's May 1950 announcement of American aid to France, as part of a global Cold War containment strategy to prevent

national liberation forces gaining independence from European domination. "By the end of Truman's administration in 1952, the United States was paying 60% of the French war effort," and by the time of the Geneva conference of 1954 "military aid from the Eisenhower administration amounted to 80% of French war expenses in Indochina." From 1950 onward the United States was "deeply and continuously involved in Vietnam." Under the Eisenhower administration American military forces stationed in South Vietnam numbered approximately 685 and grew to over 11,000 by the end of Kennedy's second year in office. America officially entered the war in Vietnam in 1965, paving the way for the introduction of American, Australian, and Korean military ground troops into South Vietnam. By 1968 American troops in South Vietnam totaled half a million.[2]

BEFORE VIETNAM: FROM INTERNMENT TO THE DRAFT

The single most important event in the personal lives and community of Japanese Americans in the 1945–65 period was their wartime imprisonment in American internment camps. Despite this, many of the third-generation *sansei* Japanese American youths growing up in postwar Los Angeles (where most of this study takes place) knew little or nothing of their parents' imprisonment during World War II. This historical amnesia within the Japanese American community was due largely to what Richard Spickard has called a combination of dissolution of ethnic community during the war, postwar economic disorder, and "psychic damage to the Nisei generation" as a result of their imprisonment experience.[3] To this day many third- and fourth-generation Japanese Americans continue to speak of difficulties in communicating with their parents.

Perhaps because of this lack of communication, many Japanese American youths, both middle- and working-class, were attracted by the idea of joining one of the urban ethnic social gangs which existed in Los Angeles from the late fifties through to the early sixties, gangs such as the Black Juans, the Algonquins, and the Buddha Bandits. For many of them, belonging to such a gang represented membership not only in a social club but also in an important cultural nexus of newly developing ethnic identity, since other gang members came from the other ethnic-minority groups. In many ways, what emerges from their gang associations is a distorted sense of hyper-masculinity and a tough-guy perspective based on street smarts and street violence. Consequently, gang affiliation provided not only a substitute family but also a sense of camaraderie that made the military a natural next step once the draft was put into effect in 1965.

JAPANESE AMERICAN INTERNMENT HISTORY: ASIANS AS ALIENS

From a small group of labor immigrants numbering less than 300 in 1880, the population of Japanese workers along the west coast of the United States grew to 85,000 by 1900 and on the eve of World War II stood at approximately 284,000.[4] The history of Japanese immigration to California, Oregon, and Washington represents, in the words of Lisa Lowe, a history of a marginalized labor force "located outside the cultural and racial boundaries of the nation" and segregated within the narrow borders of landless agricultural laborers. This history is also a racialized history of segregation, which by the early part of 1942 witnessed an "extraordinary violation of human rights" as Americans of Japanese ethnicity were thrown into military prison camps.[5]

Prior to their imprisonment, first-generation or *issei* Japanese Americans

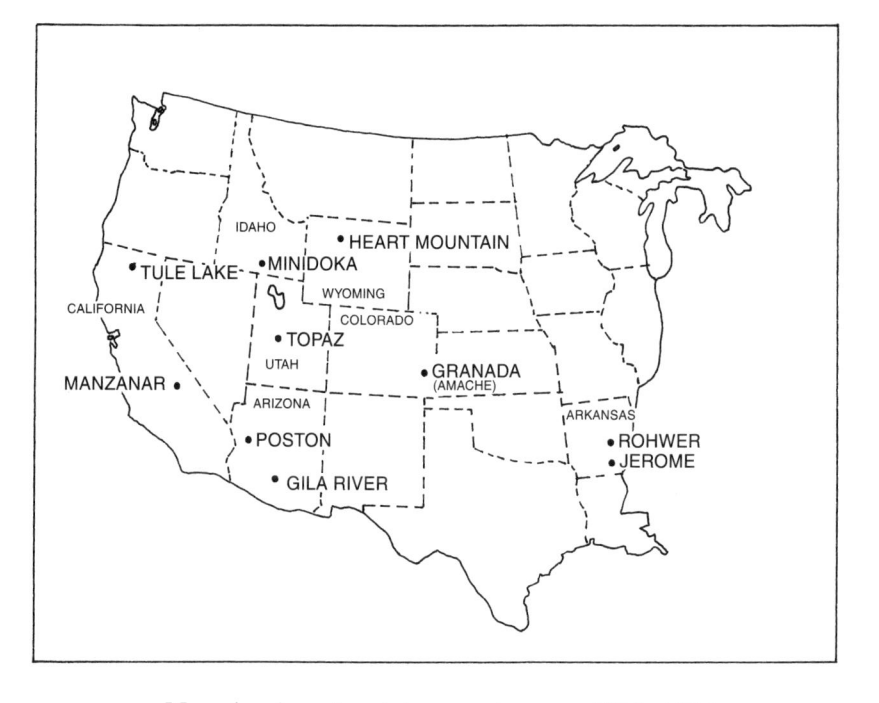

Map 1   American internment camps, 1942–1946

were marginalized and segregated within the larger social institutions as laborers, but at least had an identity either as American-born citizens or as Japanese Americans. As soon as news of Japan's attack on Pearl Harbor—on December 7, 1941—had reached the west coast, however, police agencies throughout California surrounded Japanese neighborhoods. In the week after Pearl Harbor FBI agents arrested 1,300 Japanese Americans. By the end of December they had jailed 2,000, and by March of 1942 this number had grown to 5,000.[6]

The leitmotif of wartime internment in American camps emerges as a collective and shared trauma. Eight of the eleven veterans whose interviews appear in this book had parents imprisoned in desolate encampments

such as Gila River and Poston, Arizona; Rohwer, Arkansas; Heart Mountain, Wyoming; Manzanar and Tule Lake in California; and in Justice Department Internment Camps such as Crystal City, Texas. Five of the eleven were born in various camps between 1943 and 1946. The rest were born immediately after the war in towns or cities throughout the nation.

On the whole, the veterans interviewed knew little of their parents' imprisonment during World War II. Kyle Miyogi recalls never hearing about his parents' experience: "They didn't talk to me about their imprisonment experience when I was growing up," he recalls. "I guess that's part of the Japanese culture." Difficulties in communicating between the *issei*, *nisei*, and *sansei* generations posed a serious problem in inhibiting discussions concerning issues important to the young generation.

Tim Inakawa remembers the frustration and futility of communicating with his parents as a youth growing up in the San Fernando Valley. "To this day they speak fluent Japanese," Inakawa states, "and what I call 'fractured' English; I still have a difficult time communicating with them." For many Japanese American youths growing up in the postwar period, when older generations of Japanese Americans spoke their native language and clung to traditional expressions of their cultural heritage, conflicts arose as those assimilated into US society sought to emulate the emerging youth culture of the postwar era.

Larry Matsumoto recalls how the Terminal Island Japanese American residents were forced out of their close-knit fishing community. "During World War II their homes and boats were confiscated and the US Navy completely destroyed the whole area near Terminal Island." Another Japanese American, Jeanne Wakatsuki, recalls:

Five hundred Japanese families lived there [Terminal Island], and FBI deputies had been questioning everyone, ransacking houses for anything that could

conceivably be used for signaling planes or ships or that indicated loyalty to the Emperor. Most of the houses had radios with a short-wave band and a high aerial on the roof so that wives could make contact with the fishing boats during these long cruises. To the FBI every radio owner was a potential saboteur.[7]

A small group of vets who had access to their parents' past found their selective memories focused on particular aspects of resistance and its consequences. For Larry Matsumoto, the essential story concerning Japanese American internment experience highlights how resistance by Japanese Americans in the camps had severe personal consequences. He recalls how his uncle refused to volunteer for the Army draft and ended up being imprisoned at a federal penitentiary in Fort Levenworth, Kansas. Matsumoto states that his uncle "really suffered for having resisted." Because some Japanese Americans had cooperated and informed on others during the war, Matsumoto recalls that "there was a rift in the Japanese American community." Consequently, as a child his exposure to anything Japanese was extremely limited: the language wasn't spoken in the home, little about the culture (other than judo) was taught, and the family never took part in Japanese holidays and avoided Japantown in downtown Los Angeles. Another veteran, Aaron Miyajima, told me how his grandfather was arrested by the FBI as a "subversive" and how the government tried to repatriate him back to Japan. Miles Yakao relates the story of his lawyer father, who was convinced of the unconstitutionality of the internment camps and provided legal advice for those Japanese Americans who thought they would have to renounce their citizenship and return to Japan.

In many ways, the reluctance of the families to recount their imprisonment experiences is mirrored by the silence of the Vietnam vets regarding their own wartime experiences. The legacy of the unconstitutional and unjust treatment of Japanese Americans during World War

II—untold to their children—created a sense of alienation and cultural disengagement for the young generation growing up in the postwar world.

JAPANESE GARDENERS:
THE POSTWAR PHENOMENON OF
LABOR SEGREGATION

By the 1920s the gardening profession in urban Los Angeles was already considered an "ethnic trade."[8] Now, with the end of World War II and the closing of relocation prison centers, Japanese American families sought to reestablish their new economic life in postwar America by returning to the urban centers along the Pacific Coast.[9] More than a third of the pre-war *issei* living in metropolitan Los Angeles returned to gardening,[10] and many of those who had worked in agricultural and farming occupations prior to the war became urban landscape gardeners after it. Only two of the eleven vets featured in this book said that both before and after the war their fathers had professional occupations—as a lithographer and a lawyer. It could be said that the consequence of Japanese American imprisonment was the downward mobility of an entire ethnic community in the immediate postwar years. For the majority of the families relocated during the war, economic dislocation (resulting from the loss of homes, property, and business) produced an entire generation of Japanese Americans for whom the struggle to regain their lost holdings required them to engage in some form of manual labor.

Many of the Japanese Americans who worked as landscape gardeners after the war operated as small-business entrepreneurs in suburban enclaves of the San Fernando Valley and the older residential neighborhoods throughout Los Angeles. Several of them found an economic niche whereby their service in maintaining the lawns and gardens of the up-and-

7

coming middle classes and established social elites of Los Angeles provided a means of economic survival. What Mike Davis calls "racism in the land of sunshine" is applicable to the labor segregation of Japanese Americans in the gardening trades after the war:[11] whereas some Japanese Americans found economic opportunity within the segregated and racially differentiated postwar society, many working-class Japanese American families continued to operate outside its cultural and racial boundaries.

A number of the Japanese American veterans of Vietnam recalled working as young boys on Saturdays and Sundays and throughout the summer months, assisting their fathers in the gardening trades. This was also true of some whose interviews do not appear in this book. Ronald Tomonaga tells of working in the San Fernando Valley, where his father's gardening route took them into Sherman Oaks, Van Nuys, and North Hollywood:

On weekends, summers, and holidays, I helped him on his route. All my Japanese friends' fathers were gardeners. My younger brother lucked out because the truck only had room for the two of us, so my brother would fill in only when I stayed home sick. I started helping my dad on his gardening route when I was ten. When I first started working with him, I wasn't that helpful, I was mainly a gofer. I helped my dad all through high school and became a good gardener myself.

Tim Inakawa recalls the emotional turmoil of a young boy struggling with questions of identity and self-understanding while growing up in a multi-ethnic neighborhood of San Fernando and feeling alienated from his Japanese roots. In particular he recalls the intense feelings of humiliation working with his father:

When I was growing up I thought gardening was such a demeaning type of work. I was always embarrassed that my dad was a gardener. I knew that was all

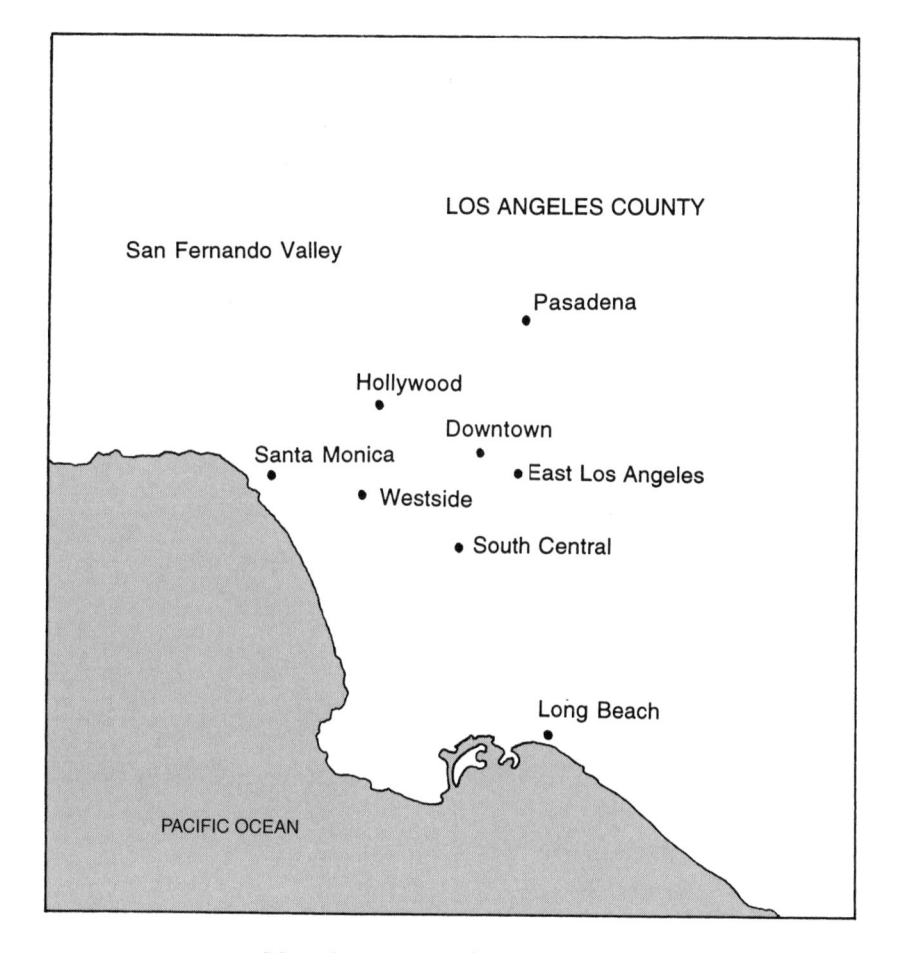

Map 2 Los Angeles, 1965–1972

he could do at the time, but I couldn't accept it as a kid. I was too immature to realize that he was doing the best he could under the circumstances. My mom picked green onions and strawberries at a local farm and she also worked as a domestic housecleaner. I didn't want to tell people my parents did this kind of

work. I went through a period where I was embarrassed to be with my parents, especially riding around in the gardening truck.

For many, the memory of helping out their fathers on weekends and in summer vacations was of a time not filled with fun and frivolity but of heavy outdoor work in strong heat. Another whose interview is not published here, Clarence Yoshii, remembers working with his father and how envious he was of his friends who could stay home and play:

It was terrible working for my father doing gardening on Saturdays and during my summer vacation. I remember having to get up early in the morning on Saturdays, riding in the pickup truck, while my white neighborhood friends would be playing outside on their bikes. Plainly put, I envied them. Most of my Japanese American friends were involved in gardening with their fathers.

Nor was there any idyllic bonding of fathers and sons while they worked: in most cases very little was said between them as they spent the day traveling the circuit from customer to customer, mowing and edging, raking and hosing down the lawns.

THE URBAN CONTEXT:
SCHOOL, GANGS, AND YOUTH REBELLION

A prominent feature of working-class Japanese American youths growing up in southern California during the late fifties and early sixties was an increasing separation from their parents' Japanese culture and a participation in the emerging youth culture of the period. This separation or alienation from the traditional cultural mooring of their elders constituted a point of departure from the norms of Japanese social and cultural

etiquette that had begun during the internment period of the war: for these Japanese American youths, any sense of identity with their ancestral lineage was ruptured, fragmented, and irreparably damaged.

In the pre-war years, Japanese American youth gangs were influenced by the Chicano zoot suits hanging out in "bars and on street corners in Los Angeles, Stockton, San Francisco, and other towns." During the imprisonment period, when parental authority either disappeared or was easily overlooked in the atmosphere of military barracks and barbed wire surroundings, the younger generation had more freedom to roam and create relationships with others beyond sight of their elders, and juvenile delinquency became a problem.[12]

Urban gang membership consequently became important to many working-class Japanese American youths growing up in Los Angeles during the postwar period. On the whole, the Japanese American gangs were not seriously criminally inclined but represented more a set of fairly harmless juvenile urban groupings. Trapped between the affluence of American society in the aftermath of the war and their inability to gain access to this affluence, working-class Japanese American youths "gravitated toward gangsterism."[13] Marcus Miyatomo recounts how his lack of interest in school led to him dropping out in the eleventh grade and participating in minor criminal activities such as intimidating other schoolkids to give him their money. Miyatomo's criminal activities landed him in juvenile court, where the judge, not untypically, presented the option of going into the military, which the young Miyatomo accepted.

Gang membership inevitably brought Japanese American youths into social contact with other minorities in the vast multi-ethnic communities of Los Angeles. It was not uncommon for African American and Japanese American youths, for example, or for Hispanic and Asian kids to belong to the same gangs. Tim Inakawa, who grew up in the San Fernando Valley, joined gangs which brought him into contact with African

American kids, and suggests that living in a multi-ethnic community allowed him to "maneuver with tolerance and acceptance across racial lines."

This intermingling of ethnic youth cultures had an interesting impact upon the styles of clothing and hair worn by Japanese American youths. Some of those from East Los Angeles, for example, dressed like the Hispanic kids of the time, wearing khakis, serge shirts buttoned all the way to the top, and highly polished black toe shoes. Hairstyle was also important in the Hispanic youth culture of the time. Kids combed their hair back in a pompadour style with Murray's Hair Wax, which was used predominantly in the African American communities. One of my wider contacts, Mike Nishiki, recalls that

hairstyles began to change in the early 1960s. One popular style was called the "Trojan." The hair was kept long, but it went on a slant. First we got a flat top and slicked it down. It was real short in the back. Some guys cut the slant so steep, they'd almost be bald in the back. We combed it straight up on the front with the long sides. On the Eastside we did the pompadour, while on the Westside of town, blacks and Asians wore the Trojan.

In the late fifties and early sixties there were three large Japanese American gangs within the greater Los Angeles metropolitan area: the Algonquins, the Ichibans (a female Japanese American gang), and the Black Juans. Mike Nishiki remembers that the West Los Angeles Japanese Americans (many of whom had close associations with African Americans) wore long black trench coats while standing at street corners looking tough. "Gang culture back then was totally different from what it is today," states Nishiki:

We didn't have the Crips and Bloods dominating urban Los Angeles in the early sixties; instead, black youth gangs formed bonds with Japanese American gangs.

They were the two predominant minority groups in West Los Angeles and all the high schools had high percentages of both blacks and Japanese.

Some Japanese American youths belonged to white gangs. "By the time I was in high school, I was a tough kid and an out-of-control party person," says another contact, David Hakata, of his youth in South Central and Gardena. "I belonged to a gang called the Bedouins, named after the nomads who lived in the desert." The Bedouins, a white gang, controlled an area north of Gardena in Hawthorne, Lennox, and Inglewood. "We drank a lot," David Hakata recalls, "cruised our cars with metal name plates in the back windshield, and fought with the Algonquins, Black Juans, Gardena Boys, and the Barons."

For many male Japanese American youths growing up in the postwar urban environment of a multi-ethnic Los Angeles, gang membership provided a sense of hyper-masculinity which enabled them to fantasize about their social place in a world dominated by white cultural images of virile masculinity. Going from an urban gang into the military was consequently not a difficult choice for many of them. For Raymond Imayama and other members of "Satan's Sinners," acting tough and getting into fights was an important element of their masculine prowess as Asians. Raymond joined the Marine Corps with other members of Satan's Sinners in 1967.

GETTING DRAFTED OR ENLISTING: PERSONAL CHOICE OR FATE?

The Selective Service, an agency of the federal government, was the primary institution through which young men were drafted into the military during the Vietnam War. For many, as has been suggested, voluntary enlistment, whether in the elite Army Special Forces or

paratrooper units, or in the Marine Corps during the time of the Vietnam draft (when it was clear that the chances of going into combat were high), was a quite rational choice based on their experiences as young toughs growing up in urban Los Angeles. For others, it was more of a sudden and spontaneous decision. For David Hakata, whose father served in the segregated Japanese American 100th Army Infantry Battalion during World War II, enlisting provided a context within which he could make his fantasy "of being in the Marine Corps" come alive. He recalled playing as a child with his father's army backpack and pretending to be a soldier; he grew up to become a gang member. Having heard about the war in Vietnam when he graduated from high school in 1968, seeing friends and neighbors drafted, the decision to enlist in the Marines came rather easily:

After high school I went to a local junior college for less than a semester. A good friend of mine, who was Anglo, had enlisted in the Marine Corps, and we went drinking the last week before he left for basic training. He kept urging me to go with him into the Marines. In the end I agreed. I checked out of school on Friday and left for basic training the following Tuesday.

Those students who dropped out of college or who were not carrying the required full number of college units (twelve college units were considered to constitute full-time status) soon found out that they were particularly eligible for the draft. Clarence Yoshii recalls dropping out of Cal Poly San Luis Obispo in 1968 and transferring to a local state college. "I got drafted in January of 1969," Yoshii recalls, "because I wasn't carrying the required twelve units."

PREPARING FOR WAR:
BASIC TRAINING

"You must become your enemy."
The sergeant was black, but he fancied himself Japanese
. . . "Smash his nuts when his back's turned.
Ain't nobody fighting fair in this war."[14]

Boot camp, where basic military training took place, can be thought of as the institutional site of training for genocidal combat in Vietnam. The effectiveness of institutional conditioning for warfare, for a new type of insurgency warfare, required that the recruits be prepared to engage in combat on terrain that was very different from the traditional terrain of warfare: American military forces would have to become combatants within the very fabric of Vietnamese society, and familiarize themselves with the intense levels of guerrilla insurgency and sophisticated social revolutionary tactics practiced by the Vietnamese revolutionary forces.

For Japanese American recruits and volunteers, the harshness of basic training had an added dimension: the mere fact of looking Asian turned them into the Asian menace—the Jap, chink, gook, and ultimately the VC. Many who joined the Marine Corps in particular experienced their first encounter with blatant racism during this period, and recall being verbally and physically abused by their drill instructors. Some heard the term "gook" for the first time, and were made an example of in front of an entire platoon. One interviewee recalls that he and another Japanese American recruit were placed in front of the platoon as the drill instructor announced, "This is what the Viet Cong looks like, with slanted eyes." (In comparison, those who enlisted or were drafted into the Army were not treated as severely or as aggressively. In fact, many Army vets could not remember any instances of racial victimization or name-calling during

basic training, and a few expressed a positive view, recalling their brief time spent in basic training as a favorable period in their lives.)

For many urban Japanese American youths, going away to basic training and to advanced individual training (AIT) was their first away-from-home experience. Likewise, for many Army recruits and some Marine Corps recruits, post-basic training ventures into the American South during the 1960s provided their first confrontation with hard-core racial segregation. Encountering restrooms with signs for "whites only" and "blacks only" was a disconcerting and even a shocking experience for young Japanese Americans for two reasons: they didn't know where they belonged in this racially segregated society, and the brutality against blacks was completely foreign to them (as we have seen, many had grown up with black friends in Los Angeles, for example). Tim Inakawa recalled the first time he went to Nashville, Tennessee on a weekend leave. Not knowing which restroom to use, white or black, "I asked someone which one I should go into and was told to use the white facility." For Mike Nishiki, his first escapade into Augusta, Georgia confronted him with the reality of Southern segregation: "I didn't know which side of the street to walk on, the white or black side . . . I had never seen segregated water faucets or restaurants . . . I saw black GIs come back to camp beaten up really bad."

In the end, military basic training produced a tough young recruit ready for combat. Outside of the eleven key interviewees, Keith Kawashima recalls:

If anything, basic training made me harder and tougher as a person. From that first beating in basic training and all the other punishments we had to go through, I became a harder and more callous person. That's what I expected in the Marines; true to my expectations, it happened.

For David Hakata, boot camp turned into a nightmare. "My family couldn't believe it when I told them I had enlisted in the Marine Corps

on a Friday night and was leaving for basic training the coming Tuesday morning," he says, recalling his spontaneous decision to enlist in the Marines. "I was beaten up by two drill instructors one night while everybody was asleep. They took me into their room and beat me up, for what I don't know; they did that routinely."

DISCIPLINARY AUTHORITY

One of the quintessential moments for a new recruit arriving for basic training is the initial encounter with the drill instructor. This confrontation establishes an immediate and crucial new relationship to authority based on physical intimidation and violence. In Ron Kovic's *Born on the Fourth of July*, the drill sergeant gathers his new recruits and tells them: "I am your senior drill instructor. You will obey us [drill instructors]. You will listen to everything we say. You will do everything we tell you to do. Your souls may belong to God, but your asses belong to the United States Marine Corps!"[15]

For some recruits, this first encounter took place even before they got off the bus which brought them to boot camp. Raymond Imayama recalls his arrival at San Diego Marine Corps boot camp in 1967:

We arrived in the late afternoon on a Greyhound bus, sixty or seventy of us, and we were all just sitting in the bus when a drill instructor came aboard. There was a Puerto Rican guy sitting in the back of the bus wearing sunglasses and he didn't seem to speak or understand English very well. The DI [drill instructor] was a big guy and he told the Puerto Rican guy to take off his sunglasses, saying, "If you don't take 'em off, I'm gonna knock 'em off." I was scared and thought to myself, "What am I doing here? *Is this really happening?*" The Puerto Rican guy just kept smiling. The DI ran to the rear of the bus and took a swing and, BAM!, knocked the sunglasses off his face. I remember looking back and saw that the guy had blood on his face. The DI said that if we didn't listen and do what he said, this is what would happen to us. I hung my head and felt really scared.

With the primary relationship solidly established between drill instructor and recruit, the process of basic training begins. One of the primary functions of training, and the use of disciplinary authority within it, is to "tear down" and "destroy everything civilian in the recruits." Christian Appy writes of this process:

Nothing in their former lives is deemed worthy of preservation. Every civilian identity is worthless. New recruits are the lowest form of life. They do not deserve to live. If they are ever to become Marines, they must acknowledge their total inadequacy.[16]

GOOKISM:
IDENTITY, AWARENESS, AND RACISM

One of the persistent themes running through the Japanese American experience of basic training (especially in the Marine Corps) was the gook syndrome, whereby the recruit was taunted, abused, and humiliated by being labeled a gook—a derogatory word used in Vietnam to refer to the enemy. This uncritical and general association of Asian ethnicity with the enemy (referred to as gookism) was for many the first experience of an intimate social exclusionary phenomenon encountered during both basic training and throughout their tour of Vietnam, and also upon their return home from war.

References to Asians as gooks date back to the American occupation of the Philippines from the end of the 1890s and the early part of the twentieth century. This was further developed into an elaborate system of dehumanizing the Asian during the Korean War and into the Vietnam War. What was most perplexing for Japanese American youths experiencing gookism for the first time was the confrontation with a sense of themselves that was distinct from the body politic of American culture and society and their assumptions of loyalty and patriotism. In many ways

Asians, and specifically Japanese Americans, encountered during the Vietnam War a double-bind of "patriotism" and identification with the "enemy" which questioned their sense of both national and personal identity. Asian Americans left behind them a marginalized social existence to join in a common experience of war, only to realize that they remained marginalized as gooks.

Thus, aside from the general application of physical punishment, Asian Americans experienced an altogether different form of abuse: the identification of their Asian characteristics as something alien, as something that the enemy possessed. Japanese Americans became easy targets as examples of the gook for drill instructors to use in "teaching" what the enemy "looks" like. Another contact, Don Mitsuo, recalls an incident during basic training for Marine Corps officers at Quantico, Virginia in 1966, where he was called into the drill instructor's room and told to wear a set of very loose black pants, black floppy shirt, and a comb-shaped straw hat; he was also given a rifle to sling over his shoulder. Mitsuo was placed on a small stage in front of the platoon and the drill instructor called everybody to attention and said, "This is what your enemy looks like. I want you to kill it before it kills you." Mitsuo remembers, "I was told to growl like a gook. I did. After that, the sergeant pulled me aside and said he thought I was going to make a good officer."

VIETNAM: COMBAT, CANNABIS, AND POLITICAL CONSCIOUSNESS

Japanese American veterans' narratives about the war stand glaringly on the periphery of documented Vietnam experiences. For many of those here, this was their first time talking about the atrocities, killings, torture, and routine violence used against non-combatants (civilian women and

children) since returning from the war, and their recollections of Vietnam take on aspects of the surreal and the bizarre as random events—such as being mortared and shot at, the deaths of fellow soldiers, the juxtaposition of the incredible beauty of the country and the gutting warfare that pockmarked it—are described.

Many of the vets recalled meeting Vietnamese farmers and civilian workers on-base, and some described venturing out to establish "normal" relationships with some of the Vietnamese. This led to an experience of the war from a closer vantage point compared with those who had little or no contact with the civilian population, and the realization of the war's traumatic and devastating effect helped to establish a growing sense of consciousness against the war itself. For a small minority of vets, resistance became more pronounced: insubordination, work stoppage, and refusing orders were occasional practices. But perhaps the most prevalent form of resistance came in the form of the active consumption of drugs. Smoking marijuana, hashish, Thai sticks, and opium, and dropping acid, were for many young soldiers symbolically tied to anti-war resistance (in a way that alcohol consumption was not). Descriptions of the daily rituals of buying and smoking grass and, for some, visiting the opium dens, provide a rich social account of the role of narcotics during the Vietnam war.

ARRIVING IN-COUNTRY: INITIAL IMPRESSIONS

There exists among American soldiers a shared collective memory about arriving in Vietnam, which cuts across racial and class lines. Vets describe a sense of fear, anxiety, and concern when stepping off the airplanes and depict their first impressions in terms of the steamy new climate and the particular smell of the new country.

The first official American military forces to arrive in Vietnam (in early 1965) consisted of the 1st and 3rd Marine Divisions, together with the

173rd and 101st Airborne Divisions, and they arrived in Vietnam by ship.[17] By the end of 1965 American soldiers and Marines were arriving en masse by commercial jetliner. Marcus Miyatomo arrived in Vietnam in October of 1965 aboard a military KC-130 transport plane from Iwakuni, Japan:

The only time I felt scared was when we were first going in, since it was all unknown. Not knowing what to expect, we had heard a lot of stories. We were all going in with live ammo in our weapons.

The flight from Japan to Vietnam was long; it must have been a good eight to ten hours, with a lot of time to do nothing but think, sleep, and wonder what it was going to be like.

For Marcus Miyatomo, disembarking at Danang and walking across the tarmac to the hangars meant his first confrontation with dead bodies, some covered and others uncovered. That experience brought home to him that he had in fact arrived in Vietnam.

But the memories were not all collective or shared. While Vietnam represented, for the majority of Euro American soldiers at least, another possibility of realizing the epic myth of national infallibility and manifest destiny thought to lie at the core of the American "spirit," for Asian Americans there was the additional concern of their ethnicity, and of their identification as gooks. This concern, possibly heightened by the fact that their skins darkened over the weeks and months to the point where they were as dark as the local population, affected—either on a conscious or unconscious level—their recollections of duty in Vietnam.

UNIT ASSIGNMENT: LIFE ON THE BASE

Encounters between US soldiers and Vietnamese civilians were fairly common. In most instances, direct contact was limited to on-base work

given to local Vietnamese civilians—doing laundry, providing haircuts, cleaning the living quarters and barracks—but on rare occasions American military personnel broke through the cultural barriers separating them from Vietnamese civilians and actually made contact beyond the limited space of the military base. Marcus Miyatomo recalls escaping from the Danang Marine Corps Air Base by placing Vietnamese insignias on his uniform and staying overnight with Vietnamese friends. "I eventually made some friends who were in the Vietnamese military," remembers Miyatomo. "I used to go off base and spend nights in their homes. I had taken to carrying Vietnamese Marine insignias so that I could put them on and leave the base whenever I wanted."

Combat troops also saw local children on a regular basis. In many cases Vietnamese children resided in villages or towns next to the military bases and so would be encountered while troops were on patrol or on the road. In the literature of the Vietnam War children are presented as innocent bystanders of the war raging around them. Frederick Downs, in his 1978 war novel *The Killing Zone*, presents a sanitized narrative of the Vietnamese children encountered by American soldiers: "Through the rear view mirror I could see candy bars and cigarettes being thrown out of the sides of the trucks. Like schools of fish moving in unison, the kids would sweep toward the nearest thing thrown to them."[18]

But children could just as easily be on the receiving end of hostility from American soldiers. Clarence Yoshii recalls an incident that occurred during a village patrol:

The villagers were very friendly and the kids were coming up to the APCs, asking for food. We opened up our C-rations and gave them crackers, cigarettes, and whatever we had. The kids were all very appreciative . . . One of the guys in an APC in front of us took some tear-gas canisters and strapped them to a small box of C-rations, so that when the kids opened the box the canisters would deton-ate. I remember the guys laughing as the kids got gassed. That was pretty bad.

Map 3   Vietnam in geographical context, 1965–1972

Older members of the civilian population were not immune, either. Tim Inakawa recalls riding in a military truck which ran over an old Vietnamese woman, killing her and the water buffalo walking beside her. Reflecting on this incident, Inakawa states:

In Vietnam we could kill the Vietnamese people quite easily . . . The irony of this incident is that we had to pay a larger fine as compensation to the family for the water buffalo, because it was a beast of burden, than for the dead grandmother. It seemed totally screwed up.

Japanese American soldiers on bases in Vietnam confronted more than just the normal racism from other American soldiers; they were taunted by other Asian soldiers operating in Vietnam as auxiliary American mercenary troops. Korean Marines, for example, remained antagonistic and culturally at odds with the Japanese Americans during their tour of duty in Vietnam, and racial conflict between the two groups often surfaced. Robert Yoshikawa recalls encountering a group of Korean Marines in an enlisted club where he had gone to drink some beers:

I was with other Marines from my unit and there were some Korean Marines in the enlisted club. One of the Korean Marines said to me, "Come here," and asked me whether I was Korean. I said, "No, I'm not Korean." He asked me, "Vietnamese?" I said, "No." Then he said, "What are you?" and I said, "I'm Japanese." In Vietnam everything was either "number one," which is the best, or "number ten," the worst. So this Korean Marine says to me, "Number ten fucking Jap." I had had a few beers and came to the conclusion that this Korean guy was obviously drunk. I turned around and walked back and sat down at my table. Moments later I see the same Korean guy getting agitated, sitting with three of his buddies. He gets up and grabs a beer bottle and starts walking toward our table. In Vietnam we carried our weapons everywhere, so I grabbed my M14 and I "locked and loaded" my weapon. My first thought was, "If this

guy tries to smash the bottle over my head, I'll just blow him away." Just then his friends stopped him, and one of the other Korean Marines grabbed my rifle and said that his platoon had been wiped out that day. I don't know if that was true or not, but the situation was defused.

SMOKING POT AND ANTI-WAR RESISTANCE

In his seminal work on soldier resistance and dissent during the Vietnam War, Richard Moser writes that the American military in Vietnam was organized into the heads (dope users), juicers (alcohol users), and brothers (African Americans). Moser comments that the "purchase and use of drugs were activities that required group cooperation and trust to avoid being caught. Smoking marijuana was symbolically tied to antiwar resistance."[19]

For Miles Yakao, drug use and an increasing anti-war sentiment occurred simultaneously. Participating in the military counterculture as a "head," Yakao recalls that the "heads were the most evolved in terms of their spirituality." They represented what he calls the "most intellectually liberated soldiers" within the military:

Before Nam most of the heads had been people who were very skeptical and had questioned authority and common knowledge and probably were already open to alternative perspectives. Maybe that's what drew them to the group of people who indulged in smoking marijuana.

For some of the soldiers, getting high on pot was a way to deal with boredom and the fear of getting killed. For Tim Inakawa, a routine day in Vietnam consisted of getting high in the morning to get through the hours ahead: "Smoking pot was an easy choice when I was bored," he says.

Smoking pot also usually entailed some form of interaction with the local population. Keith Kawashima recalls the local Vietnamese civilians

selling packs of a hundred roll-ups, "the size of a filter cigarette, packaged in plastic, for ten dollars, dime a piece." Typically, a local Vietnamese kid, ten to twelve years old, would approach the soldiers and sell the grass. Kawashima recalls encountering young kids coming up to him saying, " 'Hey, Joe, want to buy some joints?' It was easy to get and nicely rolled, like from a factory. Ten cents a joint! Cheap as beer, a dime a can."

POLITICIZATION THROUGH
EXPERIENCE OF WAR

The experience of war itself provided the foundation for war resistance, opposition, and dissent within the military. Richard Moser writes that the "military antiwar movement grew from individual acts of conscience born of the moral and political ambiguities of the war in Vietnam. The Vietnam experience amplified awareness of the race, class, and imperial politics of war, the military, and American society."[20] For Miles Yakao, opposition to the war in Vietnam grew directly out of his witnessing of how war was being conducted and its impact on the country and its population: "Part of the politicizing process of being in Vietnam was just meeting the ordinary Vietnamese people. I looked around at what was going on with the war and the way it hardened the attitudes of soldiers."

COMING HOME FROM VIETNAM

"We left Vietnam peculiar creatures, with young
shoulders that bore rather old heads."[21]

American military personnel leaving Vietnam after their twelve or thirteen months of active duty usually disembarked from a commercial airline in one of many west coast cities or military bases. The swift transition from a war in Vietnam, where many soldiers were actively involved in combat situations, to a world seemingly distant and safe from the day-to-day struggles of wartime survival created serious and often emotionally destabilizing moments of readjustment. For Lawrence Yoshida, who had extended his tour by an additional six months because he was "living life to the fullest in Saigon," the shock of arriving in San Francisco was not the shock of stress but the cultural shock of being under age. Yoshida recounts: "A group of us took a cab to San Francisco airport and we met at the bar to celebrate. The guy at the bar asked for my ID and wouldn't serve me any alcohol because I wasn't old enough—I wasn't twenty-one yet."

Philip Caputo, in his memorable Vietnam War novel *Rumors of War*, has the protagonists lamenting that upon returning home "the civilian world seemed alien" and how they felt that they belonged less to this world than they did to the other, where they had "fought and our friends had died."[22] This sense of alienation was expressed not only in the shock and confusion felt by returning soldiers, but also in a profound sense of guilt.

There seem to be two basic types of war guilt experienced by the vets: first, the guilt felt by those who question their survival in the midst of combat which saw the deaths of many of their friends and comrades; and second, the guilt of participation, a guilt which emerges in many instances after the vets return home and begin the process of questioning the war,

and confronting themselves about the moral, legal, and constitutional aspects of it.

These shocked and mixed emotions made life difficult for returning soldiers. Kyle Miyogi, for example, recounts how upon returning home from Vietnam in 1970 he became involved in the anti-war movement, but felt so confused and alienated from other Asian anti-war activists that he hid the fact that he had been in Vietnam. Melvin Wadachi also returned from Vietnam in 1970 and went to live with his parents in Los Angeles. Wadachi felt so alienated and found talking to his parents was so anxiety-producing that he moved in to the family garage:

The garage was like the "hooch" in Vietnam, because it was a little raw; it wasn't carpeted and had rough wood walls. I had taken a single fold-out bed that was almost like a cot, which I slept on for about a year. I had no running water, but I had a plastic bottle for holding water, like I did in Nam. I felt comfortable in the garage. I would eat with my folks and spend time with them—but not too much, a couple of hours—and then I'd go back there to the garage. I lived in the garage for eight months. My folks were concerned but tolerant.

Perhaps the pivotal experience for returning vets was their encounter with vocal anti-war demonstrators on college campuses and social demonstrations organized around the cities. For many of the vets the anti-war movement, with its social message of resistance and opposition to the war, was interpreted as a personal and moral attack against the soldiers who had fought in it. For Keith Kawashima, both class and racial distinctions operated in the vet response to anti-war demonstrators and to the critique presented by the anti-war movement:

A disproportionate number of minorities were sent to Vietnam, and a disproportionate number of minorities were killed there. I believe this, in balance, was due to economic inequality: whites were economically able to go on to college

and get their deferments because their families were in a position to support them through school. My experience has been that it's hard to work full-time and study. I reflect on it now and I see the inequality of it. For me, that's one of the strong feelings that I still have about the war.

The three primary experiences felt by vets returning home can, then, be summed up as follows: first, dealing with combat trauma; second, the struggle to reintegrate into civilian society; and third, the continued engagement with political activism.

ARRIVING HOME: ALIENATION AND DESPAIR

The experience of walking patrol one day and then boarding a plane and arriving in San Francisco, Seattle, or Los Angeles the next was traumatic for many vets. "Coming home to Los Angeles felt so alien to me," recalls Tyler Yamanaka, an Army Ranger I spoke with who had grown accustomed to the routine of reconnaissance patrols and intelligence-gathering during his tour of duty in Vietnam. For some, who had come to appreciate the intricate skills necessary to perform their jobs as "hunters and killers," the thought of leaving the jungle was absurd and unthinkable. For others, any readjustment to the "normal" world was difficult and ongoing: "I did a lot of things I shouldn't have done and I didn't give a fuck," states Richard Holguin in Charley Trujillo's collection of Chicano Vietnam veterans' oral histories. "For a long time I didn't give a fuck. I still don't . . . I'm still adjusting."[23]

The rude and abrupt shift in the daily routine of many combat vets was sometimes eased with the use of various drugs. "I started smoking pot to relieve the stress," says Tyler Yamanaka—a common response from those veterans whose experiences of the chaos of war and the chaos of society back home created an overwhelming sense of dysfunction.

GUILT, RESIGNATION, AND ANGER

The dramatic changes which the vets confronted upon returning home added to their sense of dislocation and isolation. Not only did they feel alienated from those of their peers who wore long hair and espoused the growing anti-war attitudes of the counterculture, they also became withdrawn and unsociable around friends and family. In addition to this, many experienced the guilt of having returned home alive from a war which had left so many others dead.

Vincent Kimura connects his return home with a dislike of politics and politicians: "The kill counts were inflated for political reasons. I really don't get involved in politics even today." Tempering this cynical resignation is Kimura's positive sense of the Vietnamese community in southern California: "I find Vietnamese people here to be very hard-working. I have a little bit more respect for them now that I've seen where they come from and where they are at now."

For others, especially those vets who lost friends during combat, a great anger, toward both the anti-war activists and the Vietnamese, remains. Tyler Yamanaka is still embittered and incensed over the failure of the American military to win the war in Vietnam: "I blame the American government and the military commanders because I felt we could have just wiped them out." Yamanaka stands in a minority in expressing his intense anger against the Vietnamese, stating, "I don't like the Vietnamese I see living here today. It pissed me off that they have organized gangs over here who kill people. We gave them a lifestyle and instead they kill people. I've told my daughter that I don't want her going out with any Vietnamese guy."

GOING TO COLLEGE

For many veterans, the experience of fighting in Vietnam crystallized their sense of life's priorities, and upon returning home they entered college and finished formal programs of study. Vincent Kimura, for example, recalls that going to Vietnam helped him to define who he was and what he wanted out of life; for Tyler Yamanaka, Vietnam provided a greater sense of direction, and once he returned to college he was focused on his studies and graduated with a business degree.

Reentrance into college, completion of a degree, and their subsequent entrance into a professional career catapulted many Japanese American vets into the middle-class stratum of successful Americans. But returning to studies and shifting class identification meant more than just attending classes and getting on with their lives; college represented the institutional site at which they came to a political realization of their own anti-war stance.

POLITICAL ACTIVISM:
FROM WAR TO ANTI-WAR ACTIVIST

Returning vets found the charged atmosphere of college campuses to be a fertile ground where they could cultivate and develop their opposition to the war in Vietnam. While some Japanese American soldiers participated in acts of passive resistance even during their tour of Vietnam, others of their middle-class compatriots found their first experiences of political protest in the anti-war movement at college.[24]

Not all vets, however, aligned themselves with the anti-war movement on college campuses. Some found themselves alienated from the movement and did not regard it as an appropriate voice for their own personal consciences. For Marcus Miyatomo, the anti-war movement lacked the insight he had gained from the experience of being in Vietnam and having

seen the war at first hand; in his view, the movement was simply a fashionable cause for rebellious white youth. It was Miyatomo's experience in Vietnam that had crystallized his understanding that war ultimately destroys the bond of common humanity which connects us all. But he found this deep, intuitive, and ultimately lived experience of war—what he calls his "true understanding"—absent from the affluent middle-class college environment at his college:

I remember a social studies class dealing with American government. Being an older student, when issues about the Vietnam War came up, I tended to be very vocal and very opinionated. By 1966–67 I was anti-war and questioned many things. On campus the anti-war movement was beginning to be visible. My attitude about this was that I had my opinions, but I did not align myself directly with the peace people. Part of it was that I felt I had the right to say these things because I had been there and had lived through it. I didn't always feel that those anti-war activists who had not seen the war in Vietnam had the right to say some of the things they were saying. I felt that these were young white kids who just lashed out because it was faddish to be that way, not because they had any true understanding.

Returning Japanese American veterans were ambivalent about participating in what was essentially a white-led anti-war movement. Having encountered racism in America, during military basic training, and in Vietnam, not for the most part from the indigenous population but from American military personnel, the reality for many was the persistence of racism at home; for some, it became impossible to escape the gookism associated with the war. Historian Christian G. Appy locates the pivotal point of the veteran's response to the anti-war movement as "class and class distinctions," but among Japanese American veterans engaged in the anti-war movement it is both class and race that stand as central pillars of engagement in their understanding of the war.[25] Marcus Miyatomo

returned to Marine Air Station at Cherry Point, North Carolina only to find that the woman he started to date was told by her landlord to move out if she continued her relationship with him. Miyatomo recounts that she was told by her landlord: "Japs are the next lowest thing to niggers."

CHAPTER ONE

MARCUS MIYATOMO

USMC, 1965-66,

DANANG

Sure, I'll join the Marines

I was born at the Manzanar, California relocation camp in 1945. My father was a farmer in northern California before the war. After leaving the camp he became a gardener and worked in that occupation until he died. My mother worked as a domestic housecleaner. After leaving Manzanar, we moved to Santa Monica where we lived for three years, and then moved a few miles south to a section of Venice, California called Oakwood. The area was a low-income community that felt very rural.

When we first moved to Oakwood, there were a number of Japanese families in the area, but as time went on the population shifted toward African Americans and then all the other Japanese families left. I would say that by the time I was in junior high, we were the only Japanese family left in the neighborhood—so I hung out mostly with the black kids. During the summers we'd walk to Venice Beach where the beatniks hung out. My first exposure to drugs was seeing them smoking grass in the late 1950s.

The experience that had the greatest impact on me during junior high

was being picked on by other kids. During the seventh grade, I had a local paper route. Two black kids decided—for whatever reason—to torment me while I was delivering papers. One day they knocked me off my bike and I reached a breaking point, whereas before I would have run away or backed off. On that day we fought, and after that they never bothered me again. That was an important experience for me because I was starting to change, to fight back, to stand up for myself rather than being the "quiet Asian" we are so often stereotyped as. Fighting became acceptable to me and, over time, an interwoven means of dealing with things as a youth.

I had no real interest in school as a kid and I found nothing positive about being there. I dropped out of school in the eleventh grade because I was ditching classes and constantly getting into trouble at school. For instance, the guys I hung out with in high school would drive up to a group of kids and say, "Give us some money," and rob kids our age. If they didn't give us any money, we would beat them up. In most cases the kids were intimidated and gave us a couple of bucks or whatever they had.

There were two sides to my youthful rebellion. One was struggling with the question of identity, of "Who am I?" That was something that I did not resolve for myself—not until many, many years later. My identity problem could be described in some ways as having a certain amount of self-hatred for being Asian—and, in particular, Japanese. My father was a first-generation American, so he spoke fluent Japanese and broken English, and he was most comfortable speaking Japanese. My mother was *nisei*, second-generation, so we spoke some Japanese in the home. It was my father who spoke Japanese and we responded in English.

My parents were much older than most of my friends' parents; they were more like my friends' grandparents' age, and there were times when I felt embarrassment about them. That's part of why I feel there

was that identity problem that was going on—not being sure what I was or what I wanted to be, or being comfortable with who I was.

My embarrassment was not related to my father being a gardener—it wasn't an issue of occupation. The area in which I grew up was predominantly low-income, so economic status wasn't a factor in my feeling of embarrassment toward my parents. In hindsight I now realize that we were rather poor. There were five kids in the family, and I was the second oldest but the oldest son, so there was pressure on me, which I handled in different ways that created much difficulty for my parents—such as my getting busted, dropping out of school, and all that.

I did feel a certain amount of boredom in school and not a lot of interest or challenge, and I think this contributed to my youthful rebellion. I attended Japanese school on Saturdays for a while, but I was kicked out for being a disruptive kid. I was considered disrespectful in school, for I refused to comply with school rules.

I was definitely streetwise as a kid. I quit going to school and hung out on the streets, at my friends' homes, and wherever. My friends and I were involved in some minor criminal enterprises when we were juveniles and got arrested. Eventually I was arrested for grand theft, evading arrest, and other offenses, and the outcome of all this was my enlistment in the military. In juvenile court the attitude was, "You're an Asian, what are you doing here? Asians don't come here. You're not going to school? You'd better do something positive."

An interesting assumption was that Asians didn't belong in juvenile court. The judge told me what my alternatives were, and one was to join the military. I didn't have an interest in going back to school, plus I really didn't have any skills in terms of a job. Joining the Marine Corps sounded good to me at the time, so I said, "Sure, I'll join the Marines." This occurred when I was sixteen, but to join the military I had to be seventeen. Nevertheless, I was allowed to sign up and take all the

required tests. My parents signed the parental release for me to join the Marine Corps when I was sixteen. They were more accepting of me because they felt that my enlistment in the Marines was a positive move. I went into the Marine Corps in June of 1963.

Are you queer? Do you want to screw me?

I still remember my drill instructors from the time I went to MCRD [Marine Corps Recruit Depot]. They were all white, and one was married to a Japanese. When they woke us up on the first morning, I thought to myself, "What the hell have I done now?"

I encountered racism in basic training, but not understanding racism and not knowing it, and being an immature and naive kid with an attitude, I really wasn't aware of it as that. Racism was prevalent in the Marine Corps and in the military as a whole, where a certain attitude existed toward Asians, and I think it came from American military experience with Asians overseas. The Asian women the military guys encountered overseas were mainly prostitutes and bar girls and the Asian men tended to be houseboys. So when the tasks were assigned to me in basic training, they were what you might expect a houseboy to do: cleaning latrines and doing laundry. I'm not sure that it was a conscious move on the part of the DIs [drill instructors], but it was their perception of what Asians were good at, so that was where they directed me during basic training. But it wasn't until I went overseas that I understood what was happening to me during training. When I look back on it and some of the things that I experienced, I think the DIs saw me as an Asian within the context of Asians overseas. They simply lacked experience with and awareness of Asian Americans.

There were also the jokes and teasing about minorities as a whole, including gays, during basic. In the Marine Corps we never addressed a drill instructor in the second person, "You." If we did, the DI would say,

"Ewe is a female sheep. Do I look like a female sheep to you? Are you queer? Do you want to screw me?" This was part of the general harassment that occurred. The more lewd racial terms would not be used openly, but if there were issues and certain recruits happened to be minorities, then it would come out when others were not necessarily around. It was clear that racism existed within the Marine Corps, especially if the DIs were dealing with us on a one-on-one basis. Terms such as "Jap," "nigger," and other words were freely used. There were enough restrictions so that in front of an entire platoon the DIs wouldn't use those terms openly. I didn't feel that there was conscious and overt racism from the DIs, but rather racial ignorance and racial stereotyping that were very acceptable and consistent with that time.

There was also the racism of other recruits and Marines, aside from the DIs. They had no feel for or understanding of racial differences. This became clear as time went on: the spontaneous segregating of the recruit population into social groups. When we took liberty and went into town, it was clear that the whites didn't hang with the blacks, and vice versa. As time went on, I encountered more overt expressions of racism. Asians were always marginalized and I could flow either way, in that I had experience and familiarity with blacks and I could also get along with whites.

Physical abuse in boot camp was very much part of basic training, and to be struck by a drill instructor was not unusual. There wasn't an effort to conceal the abuse—normally the platoon would witness the punishment as it happened to a recruit.

I didn't hear about Vietnam when I went through basic training in 1963 because it was still very remote. The DIs would talk about the other things they had experienced, dating back as far as Korea, Panama, and Lebanon.

After completing basic training, I was assigned to Naval Air Station in Memphis, Tennessee, for avionics schooling. Arriving in the South, I remember going from the airport to Memphis into the bus station; they still had the "colored" and "white" restrooms and drinking fountains. I have to say, I was shocked! I had this naive attitude that the rest of the world was like Los Angeles and that overt racism had ended with the Civil War. The movie theaters were still segregated in Memphis in 1963. The first time I went to a movie in Memphis, I went with a buddy from New York who happened to be African American. I was told that we had to enter the theater from the side, that we couldn't go in through the front entrance. Because I was with an African American, I went to the black entrance; otherwise, I could have gone to the white entrance. The issue of civil rights was just starting to emerge and those real overt barriers were beginning to fall. This was an awakening and a real education.

If I could be mistaken for a Vietnamese, then I could be a gook; in the eyes of many Americans, I was already a gook!

I arrived in Vietnam in October of 1965. We flew from Iwakuni, Japan to Danang on large KC-130 transport planes. I was a corporal, E-4, when I landed in-country. The only time I felt scared was when we were first going in, since it was all unknown. Not knowing what to expect, we had heard a lot of stories. We were all going in with live ammo in our weapons.

The flight from Japan to Vietnam was long; it must have been a good eight to ten hours, with a lot of time to do nothing but think, sleep, and wonder what it was going to be like. It was a hot day when we landed in Danang. When the back door of the KC-130 was dropped and we came piling out, the hot and humid air was awful. At that time Danang was the

main staging area, and everything was coming in and being deployed in-country from there.

Danang was hit the night before we arrived. I remember coming off the tarmac and walking over to the hangars; off to the side was a row of dead VC who had been killed the night before. That was the first time I had ever seen dead bodies, some covered and some uncovered, and it was very clear who they were. That experience hit home the fact that I was in Vietnam.

One of the things I realized soon after arriving in Vietnam was how quickly my skin color started to darken and the possibility of being mistaken for a Vietnamese, not the ARVNs [Army of the Republic of Vietnam] but the Vietnamese Marines, because they wore the same uniforms that we did, except for their insignias. In fact, I discovered that if I took my American insignias off my uniform and put on the Vietnamese insignias, I could pass as a Vietnamese Marine. I did it a number of times to go off base when the base was closed and the only people who were allowed off were Vietnamese military personnel.

I eventually made some friends who were in the Vietnamese military. Literally, I used to go off base and spend nights in their homes. I had taken to carrying Vietnamese Marine insignias so that I could put them on and leave the base whenever I wanted. Those were some of the more positive things that would occur.

About this time I started to look at what the war meant and what it meant to be an Asian American in Vietnam. I don't think I had a real awareness of being Asian before going into the service. My experience of living in Iwakuni, Okinawa, and then in Vietnam gave me a different perspective about Asians. Being able to pass as Vietnamese had its advantage in that I had freedom of movement to go places other Americans weren't supposed to go. But by the same token, in certain situations Americans in Vietnam reacted to me differently. Some MPs [military police] went around saying derogatory stuff about the Vietnam-

ese, assuming that I was Vietnamese and didn't understand English. I would get challenged by MPs about whether or not I was really an American Marine.

There was one Vietnamese ARVN soldier who worked on base with whom I formed a friendship. We saw each other on base and started talking and asking questions about each other. He eventually invited me to his house and I had dinner with the family and spent the night. From experiences such as that, my cultural awareness started to grow and I wanted to know more about the Vietnamese people. ARVN soldiers lived in a section of Danang that was off-limits to American Marines. One night, when I was at his house, Danang airbase was attacked. It was an awkward situation because I was where I wasn't supposed to be—but the next morning when I went back, nobody had missed me.

A significant proportion of Vietnamese are Buddhists, as I was, and I was curious about how their temples were designed and how they practiced Buddhism. Part of the discussion I had with my Vietnamese friend included the realization that we were both Buddhist and that this was a common link between us. Being a Buddhist American Marine was really unusual in Vietnam.

Part of the time I was in Vietnam, I was a brig runner or a brig chaser, a guard for military prisoners. I ran into this black Marine I had known for some time; we were in basic training together and then had gone our separate ways. I asked why he was in the brig. He told me that he had gotten into a dispute with a Vietnamese civilian and during the course of the argument he had killed him.

The effect of dehumanizing the enemy as part of the war psychology is losing sight of who the enemy really is. I called it the "gook mentality," meaning: if you were Asian, you were a gook—and if you were a gook, you were less than human. By the end of my tour the idea that Americans were supposedly there to save this country from an invading people became more and more a misrepresentation of reality. What the American

presence in Vietnam was doing was creating a dehumanizing environment for all the Vietnamese. Part of this dehumanization was the paranoia about who the enemy really was. I think that many Marines lost the ability to make that distinction, and that realization started to bother me because I was Asian. If I could be mistaken for a Vietnamese, then I could be a gook; in the eyes of many Americans, I was already a gook! That really came home with me, that uneasy feeling, that sense that something was wrong, that there was a distortion. Talking to that black Marine in the brig solidified this perspective, that the dehumanizing process that was going on in Vietnam created situations where someone could casually kill another person over a trivial argument.

I was stationed at Danang for the first six months of my tour in Vietnam during late 1965 and early 1966. There was heavy bombing in the northern part; we were working in twelve-hour shifts—it made for a long day. Having to keep the aircraft up while these heavy bombing runs were going on was difficult work. The sorties would come back and reload; we would patch the planes when they got hit by groundfire and send them out again.

There was a brief moment during those hectic work periods when a minor rebellion started among some of the Marines at Danang. Since we were pushed to our physical limit, and we were fatigued and fed up, we just couldn't hustle the same way. There was an incident when a whole evening shift refused to work. Some of that refusal to work was related to what was going on in the States and some of the Marines were questioning why we were in Vietnam. The work stoppage was quickly suppressed by the base commander and the so-called ring leaders were pulled out and transferred to other units. After the work stoppage was halted, some of us continued to talk about what was happening stateside. There were some real "gung-ho" Marines who didn't like our discussions,

and there were others who were questioning what was going on and why, but we were the minority. I doubt that there is much information about that type of dissent in the Marine Corps. I do believe it probably happened more than the government or the military is willing to acknowledge. I was involved, though not overtly, but I did know some of the "ringleaders" who got pulled out and shipped off to other places.

During my tour of Vietnam there was a real contrast between the Air Force and the Marines stationed at Danang. Danang was I Corps, so it was controled by the Marines, but it was also an Air Force base. The Air Force guys lived in air-conditioned, fenced and guarded barracks on the other side of the field, while we lived on the opposite side in tents with no hot water. We used to have raiding parties on the Air Force base where they stockpiled everything. We would break into the Air Force compound and steal everything we could—beer, steaks, anything we could carry—and have a big party. The non-commissioned and commissioned officers would know what was going on but would look the other way.

We could get drugs as easily as we could get liquor. Drugs were readily available, primarily grass and opium. Beside drugs, the other thing we did was gamble. We had money and nowhere to spend it, especially in the early days. It was common to walk around with four or five hundred dollars in your pocket. There was the military script (MPC) which we would use, but there was a black market on greenbacks. We would have people from home send us greenbacks, and we would sell them outside the base for MPCs.

We had to go off base to find girls. There were two areas where we could find hookers. One was Dog Patch, the immediate off-base area where the local Vietnamese lived, where we could get liquor, sex, and drugs; and the other one was at China Beach. It was a very nice beach area and beyond the beach, inland, where the vegetation was,

you could find pimps. You would walk off into the bushes and have sex there.

True to Marine Corps form, as things started getting nicer at Danang we were moved out to Chu Lai, where we pulled security duty while the construction was going on there. American companies had been contracted to come in and build a base there. Most of the manual labor came from the local people, while the heavy work and supervision were done by American civilian personnel.

Chu Lai was really a village—nothing like Danang, which was the next largest city to Saigon in Vietnam. By this time a certain kind of resourcefulness had developed. Mattresses were a premium item for our living quarters and we could steal or buy them. The construction crews especially had good mattresses. So instead of stealing from the Air Force, we stole things we needed, such as mattresses, from the American construction crews.

One time our Commanding Officer really cracked down and went through all the living quarters and confiscated all the stuff we had stolen. The civilians were complaining about all their stuff being missing. These were the kind of activities we amused ourselves with. It wasn't looked at as a crime; rather it was viewed as being "resourceful."

The rule in-country was that we did not salute. One reason was that there were snipers and if you saluted, they would know which person was the officer. There was a second lieutenant in Chu Lai who was into the saluting. Once he came by and I didn't salute him. He got pissed off and we got into an argument and I said, "Nah, I don't have to salute you." By this time I had a real attitude and I got written up for

insubordination. As it happened, the first sergeant was cool and he talked to me. One night toward the end of my tour in Chu Lai, he shipped me out to Japan and sent me to another unit. That was the way he got out of the situation. The last month of my tour in Vietnam, I flew back with the unit and went into Danang.

The day before I left Vietnam, I went down to China Beach to hang out for the day. I met a woman who was pimping and I told her I wanted a girl. This woman brought a young girl around thirteen years old. As I was talking to her, it became clear to me that she was new to this and really hadn't done it before, but her family needed the money. I listened to her and I just couldn't have sex with her, so I wound up giving her all the money I had—probably three hundred dollars. As it turned out, it was her mother who was pimping the service! From my own experience—and it wasn't that many times I was with a hooker in Vietnam—I would say she was the youngest I had seen, although I don't think it was that uncommon. The next morning I climbed on a chartered Continental Airlines flight and flew back to California.

I was uncomfortable with the white peace movement

I returned to the States and was sent back to Cherry Point, North Carolina with less than sixty days left in the Marine Corps. One night, I met a woman at the enlisted club on base and started dating her. She was a white woman and her father was a local sharecropper. I was the first live Asian she had ever seen in her life. I remember the first time I went to her place to go out on a date. When she got home, her landlord told her that if she was going to see a Jap, she couldn't stay there any longer. Basically she was told that Japs are the next lowest thing to niggers. She moved out of her apartment and rented a trailer with her girlfriend outside of town.

During my sixty-day stay at Cherry Point, there was a shootout on

base. There was a Marine unit that had just gotten back from Vietnam. They got drunk and started getting carried away. They got a hold of some live ammo that they had brought back from Vietnam, and they were shooting the place up. The MPs arrived and surrounded the building. My own perspective was that it was part of the legacy that came with the Vietnam experience—people came back and acted a little crazy. They brought back part of Vietnam with them. They finally surrendered after a big standoff through the night.

I returned to Los Angeles at the end of February, 1967. I got a job working for a company that provided aircraft support and maintenance. After working about six months I started to take night classes at a local junior college. I remember a social studies class dealing with American government. Being an older student, when issues about the Vietnam War came up I tended to be very vocal and very opinionated. By 1966–67 I was anti-war and questioned many things. On campus the anti-war movement was beginning to be visible. My attitude about this was that I had my opinions, but I did not align myself directly with the peace people. Part of it was that I felt I had the right to say these things because I had been there and had lived through it. I didn't always feel that those anti-war activists who had not seen the war in Vietnam had the right to say some of the things they were saying. I felt that these were young white kids who just lashed out because it was faddish to be that way, not because they had any true understanding.

For me the key issue that got me to the anti-war position was the whole dehumanizing process that had taken place. Vietnam was a country in Asia with Asian people, and I felt a sense of identification with the Vietnamese people. What had happened with the young girl at China Beach just before I left, the experience with the Marine in the brig who had killed the Vietnamese—it all made me feel that this war was madness and utterly pointless. I asked myself, "What was the purpose of this war?" All the lies, destruction, agony, and pain that was created—and for what?

Even without knowing how it would turn out eventually, it just didn't make sense. The price that it took in terms of suffering and dehumanizing the Vietnamese seemed like too high a price to pay.

I started to read more about the history of Vietnam—about French colonialism and the partition of Vietnam, and the election that never occurred. My readings mirrored what I felt emotionally and created what I thought was a historical, factual basis for questioning the war. Why didn't the US allow a free election in 1956? During the resistance in Southeast Asia to Japanese occupation of Indochina in World War II, Ho Chi Minh petitioned for the world to make Vietnam an independent country, free from the domination of French colonialism. The Western powers denied Ho's request and supported the restoration of the French colonial status in Vietnam. So I questioned the hypocrisy of what the United States put forth as the rationale for their presence in Vietnam—to secure freedom and democracy—when they had repeatedly denied that freedom to these people when it was to their economic advantage to do so. My readings made me a different person; they gave me a foundation that allowed me to state a position against the war from personal experience as well as from a historical perspective.

I was working in El Segundo [a beach town about ten miles south of Santa Monica] for about a year and was going to school at night, and my hair was getting longer and my attitude was getting more radical and intolerant. There were some cutbacks at my company, and I was among the casualties. I felt they were getting increasingly uncomfortable with me, because I wasn't the cleancut ex-Marine who had walked in the door a year earlier. So I got laid off, started to draw unemployment, and went to school full-time on the GI Bill.

I started getting more involved with community groups in Venice, feeling much more aligned with them. This is also the time when the Black Panthers were forming. There was a shootout at UCLA involving the Panthers and some of the conflict overflowed into Oakwood, because

the Panthers were trying to come in and organize. I got very caught up in what was going on locally.

I was uncomfortable with the white peace movement, so I aligned myself with the black movement and started becoming much more radical. The Panthers backed off and left Oakwood, but there were other groups active there and I started to hang out and work with them. I was not involved with any Asian American movements during that time; I had almost no contact with Asians. At Santa Monica College I had been approached by a couple of Asian groups that were emerging—"Concerned Asian Americans" was one, and the "Yellow Brotherhood" was another. I put them off. In Oakwood and Venice I was accepted in the black movement and I worked on a program called the Wesley House for a while, and then for the Venice Community Improvement Union, a poverty program. All along I was going to school, working on getting a degree in business administration.

This was also the time when black student groups were forming at Venice High. What I really loved was a summer program funded by the Economic Youth and Opportunity Program where we got a federal grant to hire teenage kids, fourteen to eighteen years old, to run a summer camp for the younger kids. It ran for about four summers in a row, and I wound up being the director of the program for the first two years. It was one of the best experiences I had had and I learned that I liked working with kids.

There was also harassment from the police in Oakwood. It looked like something out of Nazi Germany; the LAPD conducted a massive raid in Oakwood, supposedly looking for drugs and criminals. The whole area was sealed off and the police were there in force. They had a list of houses they freely entered, searching them and arresting people. Oakwood was like a military state; there were police everywhere. We were trying to find out what was going on and why all these people were being arrested. By this time my hair was really long, down my back, and I'd be

walking down the street and the police would pull me over and start harassing me.

Eventually, people from the "High Potential Asian Program" at UCLA contacted me and asked if I wanted to attend college there. It sounded good to me, plus they would pay my tuition—so I went to UCLA. Through this program I started to create and establish my Asian identity. I had gone through the black experience at Oakwood, and at UCLA I learned the Asian side of everything. My experience of working with various community programs in Venice and Oakwood was really about looking for where I could fit in and what I could do within the community. To this day, I have remained an active member of my community.

CHAPTER TWO

TIM INAKAWA

ARMY, 1966–67,

SAIGON

I hung out with black gang members

I was born in 1946 in a relocation camp at Tule Lake, California. My family was one of the last to leave Tule Lake at the end of the war. They returned to southern California and settled in the San Fernando Valley. My father was a gardener for most of his life. I remember as a kid working with him on weekends and during summer vacation. He was a *kibei*—born in Hawaii, educated in Japan—and returned to America to work. My parents had met in Japan prior to World War II. To this day they speak fluent Japanese and what I call "fractured" English; I still have a difficult time communicating with them. I don't think I've ever really effectively communicated with them, because I have spoken English most of my life. Even today, we do a lot of hand signaling when we talk. I think a lot of Japanese American kids who grew up around my time experienced this same problem, because a majority of the families were first- or second-generation, coming out of the internment camps.

Although my parents are Buddhists, they didn't maintain a Buddhist altar in our home. As a kid growing up in the San Fernando Valley, I

didn't take to Buddhism as readily as they did. They were very close to the Buddhist church and community center out in the San Fernando Valley.

I went to high school in San Fernando and graduated in 1963. Academically, I maintained about a "B" average as a student. In school I drifted socially and started hanging around with African American kids. There were very few Japanese Americans in my high school at that time. If I recall correctly, the high-school student population was approximately a third Hispanic, a third African American, and a third Caucasian; it was a good cross-section of people to grow up around. My family stressed education. I think it's typical for Japanese parents, even if they don't tell you, to have an expectation for the kids to succeed in school. I can't remember them saying, "You've got to keep going with your education," or, "You've got to go to college," but the unspoken expectation was that *I would go to college.*

I remember as a kid I tried to be rowdy. I weighed around 100lb soaking wet. I was always the instigator around other kids; I was always trying to start trouble. I was probably very lonely as a kid. Kids seek friends who can be their substitute family. I hung out with black gang members in San Fernando and they became my substitute family. I had the walk and the talk of a black gang youth from the San Fernando Valley area when I was in high school.

The high school I attended was a rough school and I became good friends with a black guy who protected me. Everybody fought at that high school. The Asian kids hung out with Caucasians or the blacks, but not the Chicanos. In high school I wore a trench coat to class; a long, black trench coat that only the hoodlum types would wear. I also wore a hat that looked like a little derby, which I would pull down over my head. The guys I hung out with were always trying to act rowdy, and I tried to imitate how cool they were. Motown was the influence in the music at the time and most of the cars were lowered. I had a low-rider in high

school and wore my hair up in a pompadour style. That was what "cool" was all about!

During this time I was embarrassed of my own Japanese culture. I didn't understand the culture and I didn't understand why my parents were so deeply rooted in their Japanese traditions. I had the feeling that Japanese people were freaks—I don't know why I felt this way.

I also associated with other Japanese American kids on the Westside of Los Angeles who hung around with blacks; Japanese American kids on the Eastside hung out with Chicanos. We all hung out at the Holiday Bowl in the Crenshaw district. I practically lived there; I bowled there, tried to drink beers, got loaded, and had lots of fun with other guys. We would try to act rowdy; the real rowdy guys were there, but we were the pseudo-rowdies. Gangs like the Algonquins, an older-aged Asian gang, would be there, plus the Black Juans, an earlier sixties gang. The Ministers were a younger gang from the Westside; they were a little bit younger than I was at the time. Then there were the Buddha Bandits from the Eastside. This was a time when Japanese American teenagers in Los Angeles interacted with all different ethnic groups and had a social life together.

Living in San Fernando until 1963, I was able to maneuver with tolerance and acceptance across racial lines. I don't know if the Chicanos liked me because I emulated black guys but was in an Asian body! The blacks thought I was a novelty and treated me either like a freak or as one of their own. Even today, there are a few blacks at work who tell me, "Tim is really a black man." I thought the blacks had power and were stronger than everybody else. John Wayne impressed me, but I wasn't 6'4" and I never would be—but I knew a lot of short black guys who were tough and could fight.

I never dated a black girl, though there were a couple I wanted to

date. Real gorgeous girls—they were courted by a lot of folks. Most of the ones who wanted to go out with me, I didn't want to go with. I dated Hispanic girls and I also took out a couple of Caucasians. I got along well with everybody. I was trying on new identities and rebelling against my family. I remember once I brought home four black friends after school. My mom is probably the biggest racist I know—most Japanese are, at least the *kibei* and *nisei*. Most Japanese parents want their kids to grow up around other Japanese kids, so if you hang out with any other ethnic groups they don't like it. I'd say to my mom, "These guys are nice guys," while she was busily putting away all the good china. "These guys always protect me at school," I'd try again. When I brought them to my house, my mom would fall apart, saying stuff like, "They're going to rob us." I couldn't explain to her that once you get into the group and once you're accepted, they don't steal from you. My father just laughed at the entire scene, but he was also scared and intimidated.

When I graduated from high school, most of the black kids and some of the crazier Asian kids I knew didn't go on to college, so I didn't feel motivated to go either. I attended Los Angeles Valley College in Van Nuys and remember really struggling to stay in school. I dropped out of college and started working. After two years of working, I was drafted. But until I was drafted in 1965, I just drifted around, hanging out in bowling alleys and pool halls, with no sense of direction, no enthusiasm for school, just hanging with gang members.

I worked with my dad doing gardening during that time. When I was growing up I thought gardening was such a demeaning type of work. I was always embarrassed that my dad was a gardener. I knew that was all he could do at the time, but I couldn't accept it as a kid. I was too immature to realize that he was doing the best he could under the circumstances. My mom picked green onions and strawberries at a local

farm and she also worked as a domestic housecleaner. I didn't want to tell people my parents did this kind of work. I went through a period where I was embarrassed to be with my parents, especially riding around in the gardening truck.

Although I was aware of the draft and what was going down in Vietnam, it wasn't a big deal to me at that time. Also, I wasn't aware that the government was drafting 30,000–40,000 kids a month for the Army and the Marines. I told all my friends that I didn't want to go to Vietnam. They told me that if I stayed in college and maintained twelve units with passing grades, I could avoid the draft. But I really didn't want to go to school, plus I was rebelling against my family and the "system."

I told my dad I was thinking about going north to Canada or south to Mexico to avoid the draft. I was really afraid to die! I associated the Army and the military with death and I knew people were getting killed in Vietnam. I didn't want to be a GI and go to Vietnam. If I had had a way of getting into Canada, and if I'd thought it all out and had some support from my family, I would definitely have gone. No one said, "Don't go to Canada," except for my dad. Before I left for basic training I said to him, "You know, I could die if I go to Vietnam." All he could say was something about having to do what you've got to do. I said to him, "I don't want to do that, Dad." He said, "Keep your head down and you'll be OK." My dad was willing to have me die in war rather than disgrace the family. I think it sounds like the old samurai code. When my dad said to me that going to Vietnam was a patriotic duty, I asked him if he really understood what he was saying. He said, "It doesn't matter. Just don't embarrass the family."

I was not politically conscious at that time, so going to Canada would have been for self-preservation only and not for political reasons. I was probably always a coward. I tried to evade the draft by changing my mailing address to a friend's home in Sacramento in an effort to get a deferral. I tried to get into the Air Force, but was unsuccessful. I thought

it would be a little safer and I could learn a trade. I tried to get into the Reserves and the National Guards, but they were all filled up.

"Are you one of the guys that bombed Pearl Harbor?"

I didn't have a family send-off when I got drafted because I wasn't that close with my parents at the time. We got along, but we tolerated one another more than anything. I wasn't the easiest person to get along with at the age of twenty. I was sent to Fort Ord, California for basic training and then to Fort Sill, Oklahoma and to Fort Campbell, Kentucky for additional artillery training. Around the second month I was at Fort Campbell, they were looking for positions to fill—truck drivers, mechanics, clerks, cooks. I said I could be a clerk and got an interview. The guy just liked me—didn't know what kind of skills I had—and said I could be a clerk. He asked if I could type and I lied, saying, "Sure, everybody knows how to type." I couldn't type ten words per minute! I practiced typing for a month straight and got up to sixty words a minute with very few mistakes. That's how I ended up as a "headquarters clerk."

While stationed at Fort Campbell, I visited Nashville, Tennessee on the weekends. Restaurants still had restrooms marked "white" and "black." I asked someone which one I should go into and was told to use the white facility. This was 1966! It made me aware that there was more discrimination in this country than I had realized. I grew up in Los Angeles where, whether people liked each other or not, they seemed to tolerate one another. I was exposed to a lot of different people as a kid. In Nashville there were a lot of whites, but I didn't see a single Asian there. At Fort Sill, I was in the barracks when a guy (who became one of my best friends) said, "Are you one of the guys that bombed Pearl Harbor?" I said, "Let's go outside and talk about it," in my most black manner. He said, "No, no. I was just kidding." It's interesting to see that in the Midwest and South, I met guys who had lived there all their lives and had

never seen an Asian person. It was a shock to me to discover that people were so naive and sheltered.

A routine day in Vietnam was to start the day loaded

I arrived in Vietnam in December, 1966, at a port outside of Saigon. We had been put on a nineteen-day cruise from Oakland on a converted cruise ship that had become a military transport housing 5,000 soldiers. I was sick for half of the trip, and some guys were sick the whole time. After deboarding, we went to a base camp by truck near Saigon.

Being an artillery unit, we traveled all over Vietnam. I was in a battalion of about five hundred people; we had a total of five gun units. It was rumored that our unit itself was responsible for killing forty or fifty of our own guys from "friendly fire," because our shells fell in the wrong place; I had heard that through intelligence. In one incident a single round had killed fifteen guys. If we killed that many guys with one stray round, how many of the 50,000 who died in Vietnam died from friendly fire? I knew guys who were killed accidently while serving guard duty. I bet 10,000 guys died from friendly fire. During a firefight, everybody is shooting in all directions.

A routine day in Vietnam was to start the day loaded, either drinking or smoking pot. The first week I was there, I remember asking one of the local Vietnamese working with us if he could get me some marijuana and I would get him some beer. There was one factory that made marijuana cigarettes that looked like Marlboros. They came in a pack and had filters on them. They were only a few bucks. I got mine free because I was exchanging for beer, which was free or cost next to nothing. The worker would bring me a mailbox-size box filled with pot—about three or four pounds in it—and say that was all he could get at the time. I told him I didn't expect to see that much. I had tried pot once in the States when I was seventeen and had gotten a bad headache. Vietnamese pot was very

potent and almost made me hallucinate when I smoked it. We would smoke at nine in the morning and fall asleep by noon; as clerks we could get away with that. If we were manning the guns, it would be a different story—we wouldn't be able to do any of that until nightfall or until we were off the shift. We were never really off the work shift.

Getting high was something a lot of the guys did because they were afraid to die and this helped them cope with that feeling. I thought, "If I have to go, I don't want to feel it." Everybody had the misconception that if you were high and you got hurt, it wouldn't bother you. It's like when I drink—I seem to get bolder and braver.

I think a lot of us were scared, and smoking pot helped us cope with the fear. All that most guys had to look forward to for almost a year was waking up in a mosquito- and snake-infested jungle. There were snakes that could kill you in two seconds. I thought to myself, "If I'm going to die I don't want to know about it; I want to be in a trance so I don't feel it."

There was also the boredom; there was really nothing to do at times. Smoking pot was an easy choice when I was bored. I couldn't function when I was loaded. To this day I've never smoked anything so strong; one hit and I was stoned for hours. Smoking the local grass was mind-expanding; I remember talking with other guys and we would get into subject matters I had never talked about before. I remember guys passing out from smoking strong pot. We traded anything American—smokes, cameras, beer—for the local Vietnamese pot. Exchanging American currency for Vietnamese currency was a way of making lots of money there. Selling beer, soap, lumber—they would buy it all. I was in a place for two or three weeks where we had started selling currency, but it was a short-lived experience. I think I could have made a couple million dollars over the course of a year if I had stayed long enough.

*

I saw harassment and discrimination of the Vietnamese by the Americans. Everybody was a "gook" to the US guys. It hurt my feelings because I knew I looked like the Vietnamese. I wondered what the distinction was between the Vietnamese and the Japanese. After a few months in-country, I was as dark as the local Vietnamese. I had also lost a lot of weight. I weighed 135lb when I arrived and my weight dropped to 103lb by the time I came out of Vietnam. I think it was the bad food, plus it was so hot all year round—anywhere from 80 to 90 degrees all the time. I never felt like eating, and I never ate the local Vietnamese food. I heard that the local food was worse than military food. None of us ate it. My weight loss wasn't stress-related. People who got high and drank a lot didn't eat too well. We all let ourselves go to shit.

After I had been in Vietnam a while I started to think, "If the Vietnamese are the enemy, I don't have to treat them like human beings." Vietnam was a very undeveloped country. I started to think that any culture that was undeveloped was not equal to our own culture. It's probably not fair. The Vietnamese had very little to look forward to in life. I remember talking to a twelve-year-old local kid once and he said that he could be a rice farmer or a soldier. Being a soldier, he said, he could rape the women, steal food with a gun, and make money doing that. A farmer only grows rice.

In Vietnam the American forces treated the Vietnamese as sub-humans in many ways, I think—similar to the way Germans treated the Jews, or the Japanese treated the Chinese. I could imagine how a white guy from Alabama, let's say, looking at an Asian he had never seen before, whose only point of reference is that "they" bombed Pearl Harbor, begins to think of Asians as all alike. Some whites only have memories of World War II, and all of a sudden they see the Vietnamese and think, "This is my enemy." I can't honestly say whether I looked at the Vietnamese as being fully human either. As much as I despise the word "gook," it seemed very appropriate over there. I couldn't tell the difference between a Vietnamese who was a

"friendly" and the VC. They all looked like they were stamped out of one mold. Also, the Vietnamese looked stupid to us because they couldn't speak English and therefore I think it was easy to make them into sub-humans. In Vietnam we could kill the Vietnamese people quite easily. Once we ran over an old Vietnamese woman—she could have been a grandmother—in a truck I was riding in; we also killed the water buffalo walking beside her. The irony of this incident is that we had to pay a larger fine as compensation to the family for the water buffalo, because it was a beast of burden, than for the dead grandmother. It seemed totally screwed up.

When I came back, everybody was saying, "Make love, not war"

Vietnam was the turning point in my life. After returning home, I went back to Los Angeles Valley College for two years, then transferred to California State College in Los Angeles and graduated in 1973 with an accounting degree. I was oblivious to the anti-war movement because I was having such a great time going to school when I returned home. I didn't care about the protests. I only knew I was out of the Army, I was alive, and it was like being reborn. I was happy to be home and I told myself I would never take anything for granted again. I realized that I had a lot of opportunities that I needed to take advantage of. I wanted to make something of myself. I hung out with the anti-war crowd at school to be sociable, but I really didn't participate. We got into mini-protest on campus, but that was about all.

When I left the States for Vietnam, the Ministers were fighting the Buddha Bandits; when I came back, everybody was saying, "Make love, not war." Nineteen sixty-eight was the most incredible time in my life. I let my hair grow out. Gang members didn't fight much back then. I was shocked. There was something going on that I couldn't really put my finger on during those years.

If my kids were drafted today to go to war, I would buy a motorhome and leave the country. Vietnam was an interesting experience for me, but I would never want to do it again. I wouldn't have my kids go to war. Today I'm opposed to war. What has war accomplished? I'd rather have my loved ones around me. Personally, I would never want anybody exposed to war. I don't think Canada would be a bad country to live in. If I had to do it again, I certainly wouldn't have gone to Vietnam. My conscience might have bothered me for a long time if I'd gone to Canada, but time heals things for me.

CHAPTER THREE

ROBERT YOSHIKAWA

USMC, 1966-68,

DANANG

I made a foolish move in enlisting in the Marines

I was born in Bridgeton, New Jersey in 1948. Prior to the war, my father worked in a produce market in Portland, Oregon. We moved to California in 1954 and lived in the Crenshaw area of Los Angeles. I went to Dorsey High School and graduated in 1965. Academically, I was a mediocre student. My parents never had much money, so none of my brothers and sisters went to college.

We were a working-class family. As a kid I felt our family was poor. I can remember my parents never having any extra money for things. My father worked in the produce section of a local supermarket chain in Los Angeles and my mother worked at a local market.

My parents were nominal Buddhists, not practicing Buddhists. Since both my parents worked on Sundays, we didn't attend any of the Buddhist church services. On New Year's day they would stack the *mochi* [rice cakes] and light incense. When my grandmother died, we went through a traditional Buddhist memorial service at Nishihonganji, the local Buddhist temple. On the whole we didn't take part in Japanese cultural traditions,

except that on New Year's my mother made traditional Japanese dishes while my dad and his friends visited their other Japanese friends and drank sake [rice wine] to celebrate.

I first heard about Vietnam when I graduated from high school in 1965. I had heard that American forces were just starting to go to Vietnam. Beyond that, I wasn't sure what the issues were or why we were going. When I graduated from school I didn't have the financial resources to go to college, plus I didn't focus enough on school to make college an option by my senior year. I wasn't really motivated to go to college; rather, I was looking into joining the Air Force or the Navy. I went to the recruiting station in downtown Los Angeles and it just happened that the Navy recruiter was out for lunch and the Marine Corps recruiter was available; he was a Japanese American guy. He saw me and said, "Come on in." We talked and he did a very good job of convincing me to enlist. My best friend, who was also my next-door neighbor, another Japanese American guy, had already enlisted in the Marine Corps in early 1965 with an active duty date of mid-1965. My friend had told me that the Marines were forming a series of four platoons consisting of recent high-school graduates from Los Angeles. The recruiter knew my friend who had enlisted and told me that if I signed up, I could go through basic training with him.

In retrospect, I made a foolish move in enlisting in the Marines because I didn't really know anything about the Corps. I was very naive, as were my parents, since they voiced no reservations, not knowing anything about the Marine Corps. They had to sign a release for me because I was only seventeen years old at the time. At the time my friend and I were both excited about basic training.

Boot camp was a nightmare

We were given a going-away ceremony at the Santa Monica Civic Center because we were the Los Angeles Platoon. We arrived in San Diego at night and, upon arriving at MCRD, one of the DIs stuck his head in the bus and started yelling and screaming at us. We ran out of the bus and ended up standing on the yellow footprints outside the receiving barracks. We got our heads shaved completely bald and we were packing our civilian clothes away while the DIs yelled and screamed, "I WANT TO HEAR THOSE BUTTONS POP!" I was scared to death.

Boot camp was a nightmare. I kept thinking to myself, "How did I get myself into this?" I got "slugged" and "thumped" around by the drill instructors. I was made the platoon guide during basic training. We had four squad leaders and, if something happened, the DI would get the five squad leaders together in a Quonset hut or the rifle range and slap us or hit us. It was probably a motivational tool—which we didn't under-stand—to make us accountable for whatever the whole platoon did. I don't think any of them were Vietnam vets yet, since this was only June of 1965. After graduation I went to Camp Pendleton [in north county San Diego] for infantry training.

I went through Vietnamese language school in Hawaii at Camp Smith for two months. I had taken a language aptitude test in basic and scored high enough to attend the school, as did eight other Marines. The language school was an interrogation school where we learned military terms taught by two native Vietnamese speakers and a couple of Vietnamese officers.

"Number ten fucking Jap"

We flew out of Hawaii aboard C-130s to Vietnam, landing in Chu Lai at night. I was a lance corporal, an E3, at the time. When the hatch was opened on the airplane, it was like walking into an oven. It was hotter

and more humid than Hawaii in the middle of the night. We had our equipment on the C-130s—the jeeps and personnel carriers—and we unloaded all of that. Some of the units had already been in-country and came to meet us at Chu Lai to take us back to the Korean Marine headquarters in Quang Ngai, located south of Danang. I was attached to a Marine detachment, consisting of air and naval gunfire spotters, assigned to support the 2nd Korean Marine Brigade, known as the Blue Dragons, in I Corp.

Our detachment had approximately one hundred Marines. Each air and naval gunfire team consisted of two components: the spot team and the liaison team; I was in the liaison team. The spot team would go out to the field with the Korean Marine infantry units and call for air and naval gun support. The liaison team would set up the support units; we would be the liaison with the naval gunfire ship and direct them to where the spot team wanted the rounds to drop. The spot team would call us when they were on station. Each spot and liaison team had about eight Marines: one team officer, team NCO, and the supporting staff.

We didn't have that much contact with the Korean Marines. On one of their early search-and-destroy missions we were using a flat-bottomed rocket ship, which is a very inaccurate name because it pitches a lot. The first time we called for naval gunfire to support the Korean infantry units, we had a lot of stray rounds dropping all over the place. The Koreans had their own artillery and they concluded that there was no upside to using naval gunfire.

After this, for a long stretch of time we didn't do much and I didn't have a lot of formal contact with the Koreans. In some operations, we had contact with the South Vietnamese ARVN troops. If we were sitting around at brigade headquarters, a Vietnamese who wanted to speak English might latch on to me and I'd speak a little Vietnamese and he'd speak English.

On the whole, the Korean Marines didn't like Japanese Americans. I had

been in-country for two or three weeks, and we had set up a big tent in a rice paddy that had flooded after a monsoon rain. We were sleeping on cots with a foot of water in our tent. We went out on an operation, and when we came back we went to the enlisted club to drink some beers. I was with other Marines from my unit and there were some Korean Marines in the enlisted club. One of the Korean Marines said to me, "Come here," and asked me whether I was Korean. I said, "No, I'm not Korean." He asked me, "Vietnamese?" I said, "No." Then he said, "What are you?" and I said, "I'm Japanese." In Vietnam everything was either "number one," which is the best, or "number ten," the worst. So this Korean Marine says to me, "Number ten fucking Jap." I had had a few beers and came to the conclusion that this Korean guy was obviously drunk. I turned around and walked back and sat down at my table. Moments later I see the same Korean guy getting agitated, sitting with three of his buddies. He gets up and grabs a beer bottle and starts walking toward our table. In Vietnam we carried our weapons everywhere, so I grabbed my M14 and I "locked and loaded" my weapon. My first thought was, "If this guy tries to smash the bottle over my head, I'll just blow him away." Just then his friends stopped him, and one of the other Korean Marines grabbed my rifle and said that his platoon had been wiped out that day. I don't know if that was true or not, but the situation was defused.

Once in a while I ran into enlisted Korean Marines who, when they found out I was Japanese, didn't want anything to do with me; I never crossed with any of the Korean officers. A lot of American Marines also had trouble with Korean Marines. Everyone wants to be the "baddest" Marine and our guys would get into brawls with Korean Marines, drinking too much beer and mixing it up. All the Koreans knew martial arts, so the American guys would just get beat up.

*

I had limited contact with the Vietnamese civilians. There was a laundry on the main highway half a mile from the brigade headquarters, and I would take my laundry there just to go and do something. I would sit and talk to the Vietnamese shop owners. There were Vietnamese nationals on the Army compound that I interacted with.

Whenever I went to Chu Lai, which was a Marine base, I always had to show my ID to the Marine guards; they always thought I was Vietnamese. We would have flak jackets and helmets on, and I would be dressed just like the other Marines on the jeep, and I would always be asked if I was Vietnamese.

When we went to Quang Nai or Chu Lai, there would be Vietnamese civilians walking down the side of the road with bales of hay, or whatever. The American guys I was with would try to run them off the road—not to hit them or to hurt them, but to watch the locals jump off the road, throwing their belongings into the air. The way Americans—Marines and Army—treated the Vietnamese civilians bothered me because I sensed that they saw the Vietnamese as second-class citizens. GIs called the local Vietnamese zips, gooks, slopes, and zipper-heads. I knew I looked like them and that I could also be treated like the Vietnamese. I saw those as racist acts, completely insensitive to the Vietnamese.

I also saw the Korean Marines do the same thing to the Vietnamese, too—which I didn't understand. When we would be dumping trash, the Koreans would shoot their rifles at the kids to scare them off as if playing a game. The Korean Marine enlisted guys were like animals. They seemed out of control to me and I didn't trust them.

It's one thing to kill people who are trying to kill you, but it's another thing to toy with civilians who have nothing to do with the war—they just happen to live in the country where the war is. I was offended as a Japanese American because I identified with the Vietnamese as an Asian. It bothered me that Americans treated the Vietnamese as second-class

citizens. But it wasn't so upsetting that I would dwell on it; it would happen and it would pass. I wasn't consumed by the racism and I didn't go to sleep thinking about it.

I never stopped to think about it, but there could be a connection between those feelings of discomfort and my religious background. I have often wondered if I felt what I felt because of who I am or because of what I am—Japanese American—or whether I would have the same feelings if I were Anglo. I don't know the answer. When I was in Vietnam, my sense in dealing with the villagers or the laundry guy was that they would have been very happy if everyone had just left them alone. That was my feeling then. If the Americans would leave them alone and if they could plant their rice and harvest their crops, the Vietnamese would be happy.

When we first arrived in Vietnam, our air teams were more active because the Koreans didn't have an Air Force and they would call for resupply helicopters and close air support. I had been in-country a couple of months with my unit when I heard that the Korean Marines had offered one of our Marines the "opportunity" to execute a Vietnamese suspected of being a Viet Cong—and he did: he killed the guy. I personally knew the Marine who executed the Vietnamese. He had kept the man's identification card as a memento.

The rumor was that Koreans would routinely capture suspects during a search-and-destroy operation and execute them on the spot. I remember at a team meeting, our team officer, who was probably in his early twenties, said that if an offer to execute a VC suspect was ever made, under no circumstances were we to participate. By the book, they should have been taken prisoner. I think, in retrospect, our team officer felt that we didn't have the skill to say "No." My sense is that executions were

common, just as it was common to run Vietnamese civilians off the road, or to call them zips and gooks.

Even knowing that these things took place, my reaction didn't rise to the level of outrage. The one emotion I experienced most was absolute boredom. During the monsoon, for probably three months we had absolutely nothing to do. There was a lot of frustration there and the emotions would get all mixed up. During the monsoon, the road to the brigade headquarters would wash out and I would walk four miles just to pick up mail. I saw no one except the sixteen Americans I was stationed with, and we would get on each other's nerves. During the monsoon we basically did nothing; time stood still. The incidents of running civilians off the road probably happened three or four times in the thirteen months I was in Vietnam.

Near the end of my tour in Vietnam, I ended up with an overwhelming sense of futility. I asked myself why were we there, especially since the Vietnamese would have been happy to have us leave them alone. What positive things were we doing there? What were we accomplishing? The way the Americans and Koreans treated the Vietnamese, it was just senseless. I think all those feelings were combined. We weren't doing much of anything there. I might have articulated some of these feelings in the letters I wrote to my parents, but I don't remember discussing it with the other guys there.

One incident I recall out in the field involved a shooting. I happened to go out on patrol and we were in a free-fire zone where, if you see Vietnamese, you assume them to be VC. I had an M14, the Koreans were just getting their M16s, and the staff sergeant I was with had a .45 pistol. We had stopped and we saw these two Vietnamese guys running around, about three hundred meters away. Someone said, "Let's shoot 'em!" and we got out our rifles and started shooting at these two guys. I couldn't really see that well, so the staff sergeant says to me, "Let me try." He

took my M14 and he starts shooting at these guys like they're animals. We're four Americans, two from the air team, and the rest are Korean Marines. One of our team members wounds one of the Vietnamese and screams, "I GOT HIM, I GOT HIM."

In retrospect, I think about that incident. Here I was trying to shoot someone and I didn't know who he was or what he was doing. The Koreans had M16s which weren't accurate up to three hundred meters. I'm glad I didn't shoot the guy. There were people who did that every day. When I went to Japan, I met a Marine who was with an infantry unit near Khe Sanh, and he told me whenever they encountered women and children, they raped them just as a matter of course—twelve and thirteen-year-old girls.

It was a senseless war

I came home in April of 1968 and it was an easy transition for me. I remember coming back from the airport to the Crenshaw area; it was completely African American. The neighborhood had changed in the two years since I had been away.

When I returned home, I had orders to attend recruiter school. Recruiting was horrible! This was just after the 1968 Tet Offensive, when American casualties soared to four hundred a week. I had real misgivings about recruiting young kids to join the Marine Corps, and also it was tough to get anyone to enlist. There were two kids from Lynwood High School who helped at our recruiting substation. One was a Japanese girl who couldn't get in because she had bad eyesight. The other girl asked me: if my sister wanted to enlist in the Marine Corps, would I want her to? I answered with an emphatic "NO!" I told her that women were sexually harassed in the Marine Crops and that it would be a demeaning experience for her. I told her I wouldn't let my sister be a woman Marine. So I was not a good recruiter. I was in the Marine Corps a total

of four years, eight months. I got an early out to go to California State University at Los Angeles.

I find it hard to articulate where I am today in relation to the Vietnam War. My foremost feeling is of sadness for the people who died and their families, and the senselessness of our participation. Reading the excerpts from McNamara's book [*In Retrospect: The Tragedy and Lessons of Vietnam* (1995)] highlighted how the senior advisors to Kennedy and Johnson really didn't understand what was going on there. The advisors who went to Southeast Asia didn't have an understanding of the impact of Communism and the so-called domino theory. We got involved without anyone really understanding what they were doing or appreciating the consequences. Why were we there? I don't know the answer. It made me angry when I read McNamara's book. He said it was a healing process for him to write the book, yet he only confirmed my feelings that it was a senseless war.

Since we were a small unit, we started having reunions after I returned home but I didn't go because I didn't identify with them. My feeling is that I'm a different person now. I probably didn't share any commonality with them even when I was in Nam. I don't feel a sense of closeness with the guys I served with in Nam. That happened close to thirty years ago and I haven't seen any of the guys I was teammates with.

I think the anti-war movement has been vindicated by what's happened. The young people who comprised it were the conscience of our nation. I don't fault President Clinton, even as a vet, to have spoken out against the war. I wouldn't have said this when I was in the Marine Corps. I think the change has been a long-term process. I think I saw what I was becoming: a right-wing, pro-military, pro-police person. I think I was that kind of person when I was a teenager in the Marine Corps. The change started when I was in Vietnam, although I can't pick a point on a

timeline. I'm a moderate Democrat today, whatever that is. I think Vietnam developed my awareness of right and wrong, justice and injustice. That experience has had a great impact on my values. Today I work as a public defender—I've done this for the past eighteen years, and I try to help those who are underdogs. A lot of my clients are guilty, but I have a desire to help, not withstanding their guilt.

CHAPTER FOUR

MILES YAKAO

ARMY, 1967–68

PLEIKU

I was skeptical of intervention but I wasn't anti-war

My grandparents came to Hawaii in 1885 and both my parents were born there. My father attended Loyola Law School, graduated in 1928, and practiced law in Los Angeles before the war. I was born in an internment camp in Poston, Arizona in 1943.

While imprisoned at Poston, my father, being a lawyer and having read the Constitution, came to the conclusion that the courts would never uphold the legality of the internment camps. The story of his life in camp was a person who was committed to helping the *kibei* and *issei* and all the people who were imprisoned, saying, "Don't renounce your citizenship. Don't go back to Japan. The Supreme Court will never uphold putting people in jail because of their race."

The pre-war era was a time of racism; my father wasn't allowed to belong to the California Bar Association because people of color weren't allowed to join. He was admitted to the Los Angeles County Bar but the local Bar Association, which ran the Chamber of Commerce, excluded people of color. During the pre-war period Japanese Americans were

described as "colored people." My father was a reform-minded lawyer. On the whole, he was a politically progressive person. In the light of those days, in terms of things like racial injustice, he was a liberal.

My mother had gone to school in Hawaii, where she also studied nursing; she came out to Los Angeles for her internship at the County General Hospital. Although my parents knew each other in Hawaii, they were married in Los Angeles. After the war we settled in East Los Angeles, between Boyle Heights and Montebello. I went to Maryknoll, a Catholic school, from first to eighth grade, and from ninth to twelfth grade I attended Cathedral High School. Maryknoll was a Japanese American Catholic school, so you can imagine how repressive it was.

My parents spoke Japanese, but they didn't care one way or the other if we learned it. I took Japanese at Maryknoll, but I never really learned the language. My parents were more involved in American culture. To some extent, because we were from the Eastside and the Pico/Union area, my mother was involved in the Spanish-speaking culture more than most Japanese Americans. She spoke fluent Spanish and cooked Mexican food, and most of her friends were Mexican Americans.

We lived in a two-bedroom house—with six kids. It's funny when we talk about the middle class; the Japanese gardeners were making more money than we were. My father died when I was twelve, before his law business ever really succeeded. I never thought of myself as living in poverty, but we were actually very poor.

I graduated from high school in 1961 and I don't recall hearing about Vietnam while in school. I attended Los Angeles City College after high school, since my family expected me to attend college. I flunked out my first year, in 1962. At that point my mother was reconciled to the fact that I was going to be a mechanic or something that didn't require a lot of intellectual prowess.

After flunking out of college, I worked in a grocery store for a year. Then I reapplied and was readmitted to City College a year later. Even

then, in 1963, I still hadn't heard about Vietnam. In those days, it was Cuba. I wasn't political in 1963; in fact, I was thoroughly apolitical. I became a full-time student, working part-time, and hung around with blacks and Japanese Americans. For the most part I had an active social life of parties and cruising. I left City College to transfer to California State University at Los Angeles, where I definitely heard about Vietnam. I remember reading about Vietnam in the newspapers and learning that there were hostilities there, a war was going on, and the United States was concerned because the Communists were taking control. That was my first impression of Vietnam. Anti-war activity was starting while I was at the university. By the time I graduated in 1966, the country was already involved in Vietnam—having committed troops by 1965—and many people, including myself, questioned whether troops should be sent to Vietnam. Once I started learning the history of the conflict I understood our country's concern about Communism, but it struck me that it was just more Cold War rhetoric and maneuvering—more about the USSR and the United States and China and everybody else finding surrogate battlefields to test out their hegemony.

I was a political science major in college, majoring in both English and political science, so government and international affairs were something I was actually interested in studying in school. The Soviets experienced a major shake-up in the Politburo during that time; in fact, there were a number of factors we were examining in relation to the major world powers and how they were involved in, and concerned about, these little "brush fires" all over the world. I wasn't an advocate of the war, but I was extremely skeptical of the Johnson administration's reasons for getting us involved in Vietnam. It sounded to me like another American intervention. I really understood the nature of imperialism at that time and how power was superimposed onto another country not necessarily

to the benefit of the folks living there. By 1966, I was skeptical of intervention but I wasn't anti-war. I understood that sometimes we can't have peace. The whole question was: were we going to keep out of this thing, or were we going to get involved? I wasn't so idealistic as to think that we could just go in there and establish peace. I knew that nationalist forces were working in both directions and therefore somebody was going to have to fight the thing out. The question I was struggling with was: whose side did we want to be on? In the end it was more my decision of, "Do I go into the Army or do I resist this?"

By 1966 I had seen people around me get drafted. I wasn't trying to avoid the draft; in fact, I volunteered for the draft. I went down to the draft board and said, "I'm out of school; I want to get drafted. I don't want to go in for three years. I'd rather do it now, go in, do my time, but I want to do it for two years." With an undergraduate degree I had the option of becoming an officer, but I wasn't interested in that. I have a strong anti-aristocratic bent, plus I had met guys who were in ROTC [Recruit Officers Training Corps] in college. Frankly, they didn't look at themselves or the world the way I did. I could not see myself being an officer, especially the way the ROTC guys viewed Vietnam. They were going to be the superiors, the guys who told people what to do. They were going to have more control of the situation for that reason. I saw myself much more of the mentality of the average soldier, serving his country, doing his duty, but not gung-ho or super-patriot. I saw those guys, the ROTC, as opportunistic and self-glorifying; it turned me off. I felt a stronger kinship with the working class. All my brothers were veterans of various wars—one an infantryman, one a rifleman, and another one in the Air Force. All of my brothers despised officers. They felt it was like a phony construct that the military put together to separate two classes of people, the ruling class and the ruled. I didn't want to have any part of that as an officer.

I went to the draft board the day after I finished college in 1966. It

was not without some thought. I remember having a long conversation with my mother about whether to enlist or not. My mother's line of thinking was that, since I'm a Japanese American, and since the 442nd Combat Regiment was the only reason we came out of the internment camps with any kind of honor, if I had to choose one thing to sacrifice for my people, it should be by joining the military. It's the one place we get that kind of respect, where we can prove our commitment to this country. I didn't believe that, but my mother is a true believer.

I read about the life of Ho Chi Minh

I was sent to Fort Ord, California for basic training. All of the drill instructors were former Vietnam combat soldiers. They told us what was going on in Vietnam and I was alarmed by the repeated use of the words gook and chink that I heard from the drill instructors. The DIs would say, "The gooks are out there, they're this and they're that." They were trying to get us ready for war, but I don't think they realized what kind of language they were using. I remember that the DIs had a name for the enemy. It was always "Charlie chink"—"Charlie" for short. There were two generic names we learned in basic training: one was Jodi, the guy back home who was fucking your girlfriend or your wife; and the other was Charlie, the enemy sneaking around with a gun ready to knock you off or booby trap you, or whatever.

There were quite a few Asian Americans, many from Hawaii, in basic training. We never represented more than 5 percent of the whole population, but 5 percent is a lot when there are only 1,000 guys. There were Buddha-heads from Los Angeles and a few black guys from South Central who were my friends. The Hawaiians were on a mission to prove themselves macho.

*

By 1967 the casualty rates in Vietnam were escalating, as was troop deployment. The country was sending more equipment and money to Vietnam, and the war became a big political issue. During the seven to eight months I spent in Chicago after basic training, as part of my AIT training, I started to do a lot of reading at the University of Chicago. I read about the life of Ho Chi Minh, the leader of the North Vietnamese, who was actually one of the leaders of the Vietminh early on in the war. Ho was a very cosmopolitan man who had lived in France and traveled in the United States at one time. He had read the American Constitution and the Bill of Rights, so when the Vietnamese succeeded in running the Japanese out of Indochina, they actually believed that the United States would come to their aid when the French tried to retake Indochina. Ho actually petitioned the United States to come to their aid against the French, because the French were trying to reimpose colonial rule after 1945. When the United States came in on the side of the French, it was a major miscalculation in Ho Chi Minh's career. I remember having a special empathy for Ho Chi Minh and his nationalist aspirations. These ideas were considered radical at the time!

My growing radical consciousness ultimately undermined my desire to be a combat soldier. I vocalized these thoughts while I was stationed in Chicago, and I think I was sent to Vietnam because I was involved in the anti-war movement and with the Army Strike for Peace. I remember thinking about Ho Chi Minh differently after reading about him, reflecting that his life in a minor way paralleled my father's struggles as a lawyer. It gave me more sympathy for Ho's position.

The Vietnam War was a focal point of interest at that time. I came to the conclusion, "I'm in the Army, and to some extent, I do represent my community." My parents instilled in me a strong sense of community— the idea that we are a community that is unafraid to go to war, to make the sacrifice for our country. I never feared getting killed over there. It honestly didn't bother me that much. When you're sort of a wild kid—

lots of the men had been in gangs—you are a little bit more daring than other people. I always had this notion that if I'm going to die, I'd rather die for a cause and I'd rather die at a time when I'm not a burden on anybody else. I thought about that when I was a gang kid. The best way to live my life was with some kind of purpose. I didn't have that much trepidation about the idea of dying, but the idea of going out and killing somebody in an unrighteous fashion bothers me to this day. When I thought about Ho Chi Minh—a guy who had pure motives, was an idealist, was leading his cause at great sacrifice to himself and for a really good reason—what motivation would I have for blowing him away?

I was always a skeptic, and my political science courses gave me enough information so that I could debate the issue with anybody in the service if I wanted to. I remember one part of my basic training—my company commander was not college-educated and he used to refer to me as "college man." He saw that I was one of the few guys who had enlisted as just a "regular" soldier and he taunted me because I wasn't very physical; I couldn't run as fast and throw those grenades as far as everybody else. I remember a class on political indoctrination during basic training. He winked at me in front of the whole company before he took the stage. Then he spoke, "We're supposed to talk to you today about politics. Let me tell you something about that. We're here to fight Communism. You know what Communism is like? Communism is like the Army. You know how the Army is; the Army owns everything and you don't own anything. It's, "Get off my lawn, get off this and that"— your ass belongs to the government. That's Communism. You want your mother in the Army? How about your loved ones back home? How about your sisters and brothers, you want them in the Army? Get out there and fight Communism." That was one of the best arguments I ever heard.

"We're on the wrong fucking side!"

I landed in Vietnam in September of 1967. I left from Oakland on Braniff Airlines and returned a year later on United Airlines. We landed at Bien Hoa in the daytime, and I remember seeing the rice paddies below and that it was raining; it was the middle of the monsoon season. Everything looked wet, lush green, and muddy, and it wasn't hot when we landed. I wasn't interested in the military installations—they look the same wherever you go—but the native stuff the Vietnamese had built was interesting. There were lots of corrugated awning-type roofs and very colorful signs with Vietnamese words and lettering. There were also romanized signs, a remnant of the French, as well as the Vietnamese symbols.

I was a Spec 4 personnel clerk when I arrived in-country. I was at Bien Hoa for a week and then I was sent to Ankhe. I was supposed to go to the 1st Calvary Division. I'll never know why, but all of a sudden my orders got changed, and a group of us went to the 4th Infantry Division at Camp Enari.

At Camp Enari we pulled guard duty every fifth day: daytime perimeter patrols two or three clicks outside of camp. The only time we ever got shot at was during the 1968 Tet Offensive when rockets were fired into our camp. Other than that, the place was quiet.

I had limited encounters with the civilian Vietnamese people while I was there. There were civilian Vietnamese workers who would come to the camp to do various things. We all knew they were consorting with the VC at night, but it didn't really matter. I was sure they did. The saying was, "Charlie rules the night here." I don't know how true that was, but that's what was said. I was frustrated to meet all these beautiful Vietnamese women and not be able to speak their language. Some of the

women were dazzlingly beautiful. As a Japanese, I was taller and heavier, while the Vietnamese were shorter and skinnier, at least the cats I came across. There were a lot of women around Camp Enari, just by virtue of the fact that there was a war on and all the young men were conscripted. There were some really beautiful women there.

I didn't date any of the Vietnamese women, not even close. I couldn't talk to them—I didn't speak any Vietnamese and the women didn't speak much English. I'm not talking about prostitutes now; they spoke basic English. I have to admit, they were fun to hang out with too. I knew there were guys that did that, but to me it was out of desperation, from being cut off from my normal social milieu. It was usually country boys who would fall for some prostitute in town. I was older than most of my cohorts because I was a college graduate; I was twenty-two years old, while the guys I hung around with were eighteen- and nineteen-year-olds. For the most part, they were really naive and almost anything could happen to them, whereas the same thing could happen to me but I was a little older and I should have known better.

We had plenty of chances to go out into the village, especially before the 1968 Tet Offensive. I would say that in the period from September of 1967 to February of 1968, access to the Vietnamese village outside of Camp Enari was very easy and very open. Cats used to stay out overnight in Pleiku. They got in trouble if they missed the count in the morning, but a lot of guys stayed out and we had ways of covering for them the next morning.

When I went into the village I would eat the local cuisine. What little I ate was pretty good; rice and vegetables with a little bit of meat, the way the locals eat. I never got to Saigon and I never got to any of the really good restaurants in Pleiku, so I wasn't sure how the other half lived. In terms of the peasants, I ate with those folks anytime I got a chance. I established a sense of rapport with the Vietnamese people I came across. I'm like the friendliest guy in the world. I'd go out of my

way to make friends with the Vietnamese people, especially as part of a military occupation force, as we were. I wanted to show that the Americans could be affable; that some of us, as Asians, were anxious to make connections with them and to find out what was going on with them. Doing so was hard because I never spoke the language. I only spoke GI Vietnamese, which people will tell you is like a hybrid form of communication. I can't honestly say I ever developed anything closely resembling a natural relationship with any Vietnamese.

I saw harassment of the Vietnamese by Americans. Harassment could happen with anybody—a white GI, a black GI, or a Chicano GI. On the whole, the Vietnamese were treated as underlings. It was scary because there was an automatic caste system in place. If you were a non-Vietnamese inside Camp Enari, you were of a higher caste than those outside. This was just one segment of a large occupying force. There was another segment that was fairly enlightened, or sort of benign, but with a subtle element of needing to look down on somebody. I saw that dynamic in a lot of different ethnic communities.

By the time I left Vietnam, I was opposed to the war. While in Vietnam I realized that I had made a mistake by enlisting in the military. This realization resulted from everything I had observed about the war; the impact it was having on the country and the way it was being conducted. I was reading a lot and talking about my feelings about the war to my friends at Camp Enari. I was anti-war but never anti-military. I understood that the guys who were there (like myself) were just doing their job and many of them didn't agree with the war any more than I did.

I had a conversation with my mother before I left the States for Vietnam. I asked her, "What if I don't agree with the premises of this war? What if I think that it is not a good thing?" She said to me, "You have to serve in the Army whether or not you think it's wrong, because

it is not your decision. The day that you decided you were an American is the day that you decided to do what your country tells you to do. If you think it's wrong, you do it anyway."

I remember having a conversation with her about being Catholic when I was sixteen. I never forgot it. I said, "Mom, what do I do if I don't believe in God and the Church?" She told me, "The first thing that you learn is that faith is a gift. There are some things in this world that you just don't question. You're Catholic and you live by the rules, and that's the way it works." I told her that my life would be a lot simpler if I could think like her. She was basically saying that the Japanese American population has a unique history in this country because the way we vindicated ourselves was through military service. She said, "It's one thing if you're from any other culture, but the way we got out of the internment camps and established ourselves as fully participating citizens was through the efforts of the 442nd."

For me, part of the politicizing process of being in Vietnam was just meeting the ordinary Vietnamese people. I looked around at what was going on with the war and the way it hardened the attitudes of soldiers. I looked at the way it affected race relations. When I first come in-country, everybody taunted me because I was going to be here a whole year; the short-timers taunt the new guys. I wasn't one of those guys but I was in the group and I was talking out against this war, saying, "This is really a bullshit war," and, "When I get out of here, I'm going to go back and join the anti-war protesters." Once, this guy jumped up and said, "You fucking gook," and took a punch at me. His friends jumped up and pulled him away. Luckily he missed! He was a white guy and he actually apologized after that. He was an okay guy, but he let something that was under the surface come to the surface real quick, and it had to do with my race. He could accept the perspective I verbalized coming from

anybody else, but he wouldn't accept it coming from an Asian American. It was the first and only time I was ever attacked by anybody in the Army. If he had hit me, I'm sure I would have gone down. Afterward he told me that it was the first time he'd ever swung at a guy and not taken him down. I remember he was a big, giant, white boy; he looked like he played football for the Detroit Lions. This took place in the hooch, while we were sitting around playing cards, drinking, talking, and just bullshitting.

Everybody complained about the Army, but I complained about the war. I said stuff like, "We should never have gotten involved in this thing in the first place. We're on the wrong fucking side!" Honestly, I don't know how much of that came from "sad sack" disillusionment with the Army and how much from true political awareness. The process of education that I started in the Army, and even before that—such as learning the history of Vietnam and trying to find a political perspective that made sense to me—has never changed. I've always tried to listen to both sides of an argument and get as much data as I can.

During my time in Vietnam I was considered a "head," meaning: I smoked grass. Grass was easy to get and it was inexpensive and powerful. Often, when everybody else was sleeping, I'd be working and I'd go out and see the montagnards and consort with them by trading C-rations for a bag of dope. Sometimes they would trade regular cigarettes for a whole bag of grass; it was just chopped off a branch and stuffed into a bag. The montagnards—the indigenous, mountain, and tribal peoples of Vietnam— were growing and smoking grass openly; what's the Army going to do? I wouldn't roll the grass because I didn't have rolling papers; instead, I used a pipe. We smoked mostly in the barracks. Rarely did we find a guy smoking out at a bunker; that's combat contact. If we didn't want to smoke in the barracks, we went out to one of the internal bunkers

between the barracks. Sometimes we'd just sit out on top of the bunkers and smoke.

The heads were a minority. We associated with each other but we were still part of other groups. I also hung with the "juicers," the drinkers, because they accepted me; most of my friends were drinkers, actually. Some of them were religious cats who couldn't see smoking grass. The heads were the most evolved in terms of their spirituality. They had already concocted notions of war-free worlds and the idea that there had to be alternative, non-violent solutions to all these other things. We decided it was going to be much harder to find non-violent means of conflict resolution.

The heads were the most intellectually liberated soldiers from all the military indoctrination. Before Nam most of the heads had been people who were very skeptical and had questioned authority and common knowledge and probably were already open to alternative perspectives. Maybe that's what drew them to the group of people who indulged in smoking marijuana. It's not like we did it all the time, because we couldn't get the stuff all the time. I remember going for months and months without the stuff, and then all of a sudden somebody would come back with a big bag and all of us would get loaded.

I don't know if getting loaded was part of the politicizing transformation. That's hard to say. I honestly can't say that that was the case. I listened to rock-and-roll music a lot while in Nam. The two hottest albums were "Sgt. Pepper's Lonely Heart's Club Band" by the Beatles and the Doors' "Light My Fire." Motown was something I was brought up with. I remember the song, "Reach Out," by the Four Tops; we would be standing in formation and cats would be singing that song. People would be humming tunes; music was always in the background. The "Summer of Love" stuff was prevalent in Vietnam at the time.

My military service was an unfortunate footnote

I rotated out of Vietnam at Cam Ranh Bay and landed in Seattle, Washington and went to Fort Lewis, Washington for processing out. I was there for three or four days. After that I was out, took a plane to Los Angeles, called up some friends, and they took me back home.

While I was in Vietnam I heard from my friends what was happening stateside. I had no idea that the counterculture was pervasive until I came home in September of 1968. I remember that hairstyles were so different. Within a week or two after returning home I was enrolled in law school. I had applied to UCLA in September of 1967 and was accepted while in Nam. I started law school the fall quarter of 1968. UCLA was humming with anti-war activity, and many of the students were really hostile toward me because I looked like a soldier with my short hair. I got nothing but negative reactions from students, but it wasn't racial. They assumed I was a fascist and a murderer; nothing could have been further from the truth in my experience. I was ready to join the anti-war movement, but I couldn't get past that initial resentment and rage that they had toward ex-soldiers. Instead, I just hung around with other students who were ex-GIs. There were four or five of us in my class at UCLA in the law department. A couple were retired Army colonels and a couple ex-GIs like myself. I graduated from law school in 1971.

I didn't get involved with *Gidra* (a left, progressive newspaper of the Los Angeles Japanese American community) until 1970–71. I used to hang out there and, as a matter of fact, they considered me a disruptive influence there because I only wanted to party and have a good time, while everyone else had work to do. I joined the anti-war movement through the Vietnam Veterans Against the War [VVAW] and was active with them through demonstrations.

I also got active in organizing law students at UCLA. We started an Asian American Law Students Association and decided to try to initiate

affirmative action for Asian Americans. Law student associations were already in existence for blacks, Chicanos, and Native Americans, but not for Asian Americans. There were nine Asian Americans in my class, and two in the next upcoming class. It wasn't until 1969 that we decided we had to do something, that it was unacceptable to have that few, given the community that needed to be served. The number one priority was to institute a minority affirmative action program, in which entrance to the program became a central issue: we wanted the student organization to have a certain amount of input with respect to the candidates being selected for this education. It took all of 1969 and most of 1970 to get that done. Finally, in 1970 the program was implemented. As a matter of fact, the guy who later became my law partner was one of the first people we picked as an Asian American in the Equal Opportunity Program.

If nothing else, I would like my experience to give the message that people do have choices and that choosing not to go to war is an honorable choice. Draft counselors could have been used to greater benefit to this country—more than I was with my couple of years of service—by showing people that there is another way, maybe even a more spiritually evolved way, of coping with national disagreements. I still believe that there are more peaceful, more humanistic ways than war to solve problems. In terms of the broad sweep of my life and what I would like it to count for and stand for, my military service was an unfortunate footnote. I'd like to think that we all have some duty to our country that we fulfill any way we can, but I think you can fulfill your duty to your country absolutely as well and as courageously as a protester, as a dissenter, and as a conscientious objector.

CHAPTER FIVE

VINCENT KIMURA

ARMY, 1968–69

DONG TAM

My family was supportive of my decision to become a conscientious objector

My parents were born in California, second-generation, but at an early age they returned to Japan for their education and then came back to California in their late teens. Prior to the war my father and his brother operated a truck farm on land that they leased in the Marina del Rey area. When the war came, they were forced to leave their business and everything they owned; they were relocated to Gila River internment camp in Arizona, where I was born in 1943.

My parents told me that when they were relocated to Gila River, they were only allowed to take what they could carry. In 1945, when the war ended, they were released from camp and went to work picking plums and grapes in the large orchard groves at Lodi, California. We stayed in Lodi until I was about five years old, after which my family moved to Lomita, California, where my father started his gardening business. He remained a gardener until the late 1960s, when he went to work for California State University as a groundskeeper;

my mother worked in a nursery, growing celery for replanting in the fields.

My parents were raised as Buddhists, but they didn't attend any of the local Buddhist churches or practice Buddhism within the home. As a child my parents took me to a Christian church. I grew up as a Christian. The funny thing is that my parents never converted. My religious upbringing, plus my own interest in both Buddhism and Christianity, played a pivotal role in my decision to become a conscientious objector during the Vietnam war.

Scholastically I was an above-average student, and graduated from high school in the winter of 1962. I went to California State College at Long Beach immediately out of high school. I was eighteen years old and I didn't have any clear sense of what I wanted to do with my life. For some vague reason I decided to become an engineering major. I goofed around and socialized more than I should have and therefore didn't do well academically. I hung out with my friends and we cruised together and had lots of fun. It wasn't because I wasn't smart; rather, I wasn't motivated to study. I was the first member of my family to go to college—and the first to be kicked out of college.

In 1962 the American public still didn't know much about Vietnam. When John Kennedy became president the focus was on Laos, not Vietnam. I wasn't really keeping up with worldwide affairs at that time. I was more intent on what I was doing in college and, besides, at the age of twenty, everything was new and wonderful and I wanted to explore things.

When I was a senior in high school and a freshman in college, I became involved with the Gardena Buddhist church. By 1964 I was president of the Young Buddhist Association at that church. I really didn't get that deeply into Buddhism as a religion; I was more in tune with its philosophical aspects—its practical approach to life.

While attending California State College in Long Beach, I worked on the weekends and during summer break at the nursery in Carson where I had worked since high school. I helped with the planting and watering and sometimes assisted in sales. I had helped my dad on his gardening route, but once I started working at the nursery I didn't have time to do that too.

By my third year of college my grades had dropped so low that I was expelled. I took UCLA Extension classes to try to bring my GPA [grade point average] up so I could get back into college, but for some reason I didn't do well. I attribute my failure in college to my lack of motivation and playing around too much. Finally, I dropped out of college completely and got a job at an engineering company. I worked there one year prior to being drafted.

I filed for my conscientious objector status prior to being drafted. My family was supportive of my decision to become a CO. First of all, I didn't think we should be in Vietnam. From a political and ethical standpoint, I was against the war in Vietnam, though I wasn't opposed to all wars. From watching television news, I couldn't understand why we were fighting a war in Vietnam. I wasn't a political radical. My other Japanese Americans friends felt a lot of ambivalence concerning the war, as I recall. As long as the war didn't affect them, they didn't voice strong feelings one way or the other. Once I became eligible for the draft, I felt more strongly opposed to the war. By 1966–67 I was no longer active in the Gardena Buddhist church. As a Buddhist, I didn't want to participate in killing anybody and, in return, I didn't want to get killed.

There are two types of conscientious objector. One says, "I'm not going to carry a weapon and I'm not going to serve in the US Armed Forces." Those people have the choice of sticking around and getting caught and possibly jailed, or fleeing to Canada and possibly never coming

back. I didn't want to leave the US. The alternative choice says, "I will serve in the Armed Services, but I will not carry a weapon." This is the position I chose as a CO. Another reason for my being a CO was that if I was sent to Vietnam as a regular combat troop, being an Asian American I could easily be mistaken for the so-called enemy. Where does that put me? It was a unique situation for the Japanese Americans who served in the Vietnam War. The final reason for opposing the war was just plain fear. I didn't want to go to war and I didn't want to get killed, period.

I believed in the ideas of freedom, liberty, and equality and was opposed to Communism, as we knew it then. But I wondered how the events in Vietnam 13,000 miles away could possibly affect Americans at home. Maybe my perspective was too narrow and naive and perhaps I didn't have all the facts, but I didn't buy the argument that this particular war concerned Communism versus freedom. After I arrived in Vietnam, to be blunt, I became even more politically opposed to the war.

I refused to even train with weapons

I was in the Army from 1967 to 1969. My total time in service was twenty-one months. When I first got drafted I was sent to Fort Ord, California, but was there only three or four days before I was shipped to Fort Sam Houston in San Antonio, Texas, where all COs were sent for training. The reason I left Fort Ord was because basic training there included weapons training. I refused to even train with weapons as a CO; I never carried or fired a weapon the entire time of my service. I was with other COs (there were quite a few Seventh Day Adventists who were COs) but we didn't talk too much about why we were objectors during basic.

War's hell; I just did my job as a medic

I received orders to go to Vietnam in the spring of 1968. I flew out from Travis Air Force Base to Guam, landing at Tan Son Nhut air base outside of Saigon. I arrived in Vietnam around April of 1968, during the dry season. I was transported to Dong Tam, approximately forty kilometers southwest of Saigon, base camp of the Army Mobile Riverine Force. I went through jungle training and from there I was assigned to the USS *Mercer*, which operated on the Mekong River delta and belonged to the "River Rats." I also went on patrols on the Mekong River for about six months.

At Dong Tam, my commanding officer assumed that I was supposed to receive a weapon. I told him I wouldn't carry a weapon because I was a CO, and they were surprised. They tried to have me carry a weapon, but I refused. I had assumed that they would know I was a CO and wouldn't carry a weapon, and the fact that they questioned my CO status was surprising to me. I never carried a gun, but I did carry a bayonet to cut open coconuts!

On patrols we would come across small villages and occasionally I had contact with the villagers, who would come up to me and speak Vietnamese, assuming I was Vietnamese. Each company on patrol usually had a Vietnamese interpreter and since I didn't carry a weapon, the villagers probably thought I was the interpreter.

Typically during our patrols, we walked in a single line spaced approximately five yards apart—the idea being that a clump of people would be more exposed to ambush than a loosely spread-out cluster. The medic walked in the middle of the platoon. We did a lot of patrols. I got a medal after being in the field for six months—an air medal with oak leaf cluster—signifying that I had been on at least fifty helicopter flights. In addition to the foot patrols, I went out on the riverboat patrols that

usually took two to four days; we walked through scattered villages in the delta region of the Mekong. Most of the region was covered by lush rice paddies surrounded by thick jungle and large areas that were burnt by napalm.

As a medic, most of the injuries I treated out in the field during the patrols were injuries resulting from booby traps. Many of the booby traps were constructed from converted 105mm howitzer rounds fired by US forces that failed to explode; other types of traps used frag grenades. Relatively speaking, I was lucky because the policy at that time was that medics were out in the field for six months; the second six months we were in aid stations located in the rear.

Once while on patrol, two guys in my platoon were killed in an ambush. My platoon happened to be in the lead of a company sweep through the Mekong delta region known as the "Plain of Reeds." The point man was hit by a booby trap and one of the others close to the front was shot in the chest. That was the worst experience I had during my time in Nam. On this patrol I noticed mounds of mud that were in places where people would seek shelter from bombs. I was walking along with the platoon and those mounds happened to be wet, which meant they had been made recently. I should have known better. It meant that there was probably enemy in the area. That's when we were ambushed and the two guys died. That was the scariest time in my life. War's hell; I just did my job as a medic.

I don't recall any burning of empty villages during any of the patrols I went on. I witnessed our guys shooting the livestock, but most of the time we would never see the Viet Cong, even when we were ambushed. The typical way we would operate was that if we were ambushed the soldiers were trained to put out the fire power without knowing where the target was. All I did was hope that nobody got hurt. If someone did get hurt, I would have to run to wherever the person was hit. I saw

people die and I saw people get maimed. When you're in a firefight and somebody gets injured, you never forget the smell of blood; it's kind of a burnt, weird smell.

My first experience with combat was when we were ambushed and one guy needed a medic. Something was wrong with his weapon and he got powder burns in his eyes. I didn't know that at the time. He was lying in water and I went over to him, while bullets whizzed by. I determined that he wasn't hit and put his head down. That was my platoon's first experience of knowing that I could respond to an emergency. After that, there were no problems. It really wasn't hard to persevere as a CO, because once the platoon had confidence in my abilities as a medic they did everything for me. Especially being a medic in the field, I could be the one who saved one of the infantry guys' lives.

I really felt a part of the platoon. I was respected by the guys and they backed me up. They all wanted to survive. I don't recall too many gung-ho guys there. I do recall that there was a lot of waste. When I was on the river patrols, we would be coming back from patrol and the guys would throw their ammo in the water so that they would have less weight to carry. They would get new stuff the next time they went out. Another tragedy was the kill count. When we went out on patrol, our officers would report so many Viet Cong killed even if we hadn't encountered one. These reports were given to the colonel sitting in the chopper above us, who wanted a good kill count so that he could have a good record.

There were civilian casualties among local people. One time I gave aid to our interpreter during a firefight. Two other infantry guys were hurt. The closest one to me was the interpreter, so I started with him. I was told to take care of our guys first, so that's what I did. I never gave aid to local Vietnamese civilians. I saw a lot of Vietnamese who had prior injuries or were deformed in some way. They had gone through many,

many years of war with the Japanese, the French, and whoever else was there.

The second six months as a medic I was in a battalion aid station with the 47th Infantry near Ben Luc. I happened to be the battalion medical records clerk, so I kept statistics and took people in. During the first six months, when I was out in the field, I don't recall women being available. In the second six months, when I was stationed at the aid station, we had a steam bath where we could get a nude massage on base. Actually, it was more than a massage. Being a medic, I had to check out the girls hired to come on the base to make sure they didn't have gonorrhea or syphilis. The steam room was open during the daytime. I don't think it cost that much. These women also worked as maids, cleaning and doing laundry. I had one girl whom I paid to clean my area and do my laundry. There was a barber shop on base, and the barbers were all Vietnamese. There was a small village adjacent to the aid station; I never went there. I never went off base. Everything was provided on base.

Being in Vietnam really opened my eyes. As an American, I realized how much we have it made back in the US. One of the things I thought about was wishing I could go to a supermarket and stroll through the aisles, picking whatever I wanted for my dinner. The Mekong region is principally an agricultural area with no TV, no electricity, no nothing. The houses were thatch huts; villagers slept on raised wooden platforms with hogs going through the house. It was a very primitive agricultural area. When I say this, I'm not judging them as a people. They haven't seen the other side, so for them it's okay. That was something I learned for myself: don't judge other people's culture or society. That's all they know and they're happy with it. I didn't really talk about this kind of thing with the guys. The main focus for everyone was to get back in one piece.

I was more opposed to the war once I got to Vietnam. I saw a lot of hypocrisy and waste. The kill count is one example. I'm sure people watching the news back home were thinking we were doing a good job. Look at how many Americans died in Vietnam—more than 50,000. I kept these feelings inside. I am proud to have been a CO and to have never carried a weapon. That was my only way of protesting what I stood for. They sent me to a place for a cause I thought was wrong. Not carrying a weapon reinforced my convictions. I believed that I had to work within the system. I avoided getting into deep discussions about the war with other Americans in Vietnam. "The war sucked," was how everyone put it. I think this sentiment was shared by many of the guys, but it wasn't verbalized; it was basically understood. What the politicians in the US were saying, versus the reality of what was going on and the attitude of the guys, was completely different. I didn't personally run into gung-ho pro-military guys. Most of them tried to do their job. I was twenty-five years old when I was in Vietnam; I was old compared to the youthful eighteen- and nineteen-year-old draftees. I felt sorry for them because I didn't think they were mature enough to deal with the trauma of war. Maybe that's why I survived without any big problems when I got back.

I don't think I'm such a great moral person

I served twelve months in-country. I left Vietnam in 1969 on a Pan-Am flight that took me to San Francisco. I got an early release to return to school at California State College at Long Beach. This is one part I really don't talk too much about, and that's why I have a hard time remembering it. Maybe I try to block it out. I came back here and a lot of Vietnam vets had Post-Traumatic Stress Disorder [PTSD]. I don't think I ever went through that, but I have encountered some vets who have. I was just so happy to come home in one piece. I learned a lot over there.

After I came back to the States, I had additional time to do on my enlistment and I was supposed to go back east somewhere. I took about a one-week leave and, during that time, I went to visit my family in Los Angeles. While I was home I went to Fort McArthur in San Pedro, to their personnel department, and looked at their board. It showed an opening for a medic. I asked that my orders be changed so I could work in the hospital there at San Pedro. I was reassigned to the hospital and I lived at my parents' home. I was there for probably three months. It was like being a medical assistant. During that time, I had put in a request for an early discharge to go back to school, and it was granted.

By 1969 the anti-war movement was quite strong. That surprised me; I'd been gone almost two years. When I got back to Cal State Long Beach, new courses had been added. The Asian American movement was very strong, as were the African American and Chicano movements. In order for me to graduate, I needed to bring my GPA up. I took as many Asian American classes as possible. It brought me up to date on what that movement was about and I earned higher grades. The guys with long hair really freaked me out. I never grew my hair long. There was more anti-Vietnam sympathy among the campus students than I could handle. I didn't really care to get involved in politics or political movements. I was just happy to get back and I was really focused on finishing my degree. While I was in Vietnam, I realized what happened in terms of my education; I had done poorly in school, which got me kicked out and drafted into the Army. Why? The answer was that I was not motivated and therefore not focused on my studies.

My focus became getting my degree and being happy and appreciative to be alive and back here. I think the twelve months in Vietnam was a maturing, awakening experience. I asked myself, "What am I doing for myself? What do I want? What is life about? What's important to me?" I am basically conservative and not extreme. There were things in the Asian American movement I believed in and other things that I thought

were just trendy. I didn't think about whether or not filing for CO status was a conservative thing to do. It was just the logical decision and the middle road for me to take in response to the war. I'm a middle-of-the-roader, really. I think that most people don't want to kill; most people are good. But forced into a situation where you get killed or you kill, I think most people don't want to get killed. I didn't want to be put in that position. I don't think I'm such a great moral person. I would do it again in the same situation. I feel good about having made the choice to be a CO. I'm neither ashamed nor proud of being a CO; it's just the way it was.

I think there were some very positive things about having served in Vietnam. It helped me define who I was and what I wanted. I think it gave me a better appreciation of what we have here in the US. It gave me the opportunity to go to Japan. I don't know if this is a positive, but I learned that I don't like politics and politicians. The kill counts were inflated for political reasons. I really don't get involved in politics even today. I hate to be this way, but I don't give a shit, unless it's a local issue.

On the negative side, I feel bad about war in general and people getting killed for the ideals of that particular war. Now I live in Long Beach, with Little Saigon fairly close, and I'm sure there's a lot of animosity toward the Vietnamese from the people who live in the area. I think that's part of life. It's like the Japanese. There was a lot of animosity after World War II. You can't do anything about those things. I find Vietnamese people here to be very hard-working. I have a little bit more respect for them now that I've seen where they come from and where they are at now. I think they are a happy people living here in America. It hasn't been as bad for me as for some of the other guys who faced problems with Agent Orange and Post-Traumatic Stress Disorder and all the other problems they've had. I feel quite fortunate in coming home from the war in one piece.

CHAPTER SIX

RAYMOND IMAYAMA

USMC, 1968–69

DONG HA

My parents thought being in the military would straighten my ass out

My father was born in Utah, moved with his family to Hiroshima, Japan before World War II, and returned to California, settling in South Pasadena where he attended high school. My dad was at a football game at South Pasadena High School when the announcement came over the loudspeaker that Japan had bombed Pearl Harbor. My grandfather on my dad's side was a gardener in West Los Angeles before the war. My mother's family had a farm in Santa Barbara, where she was born.

My parents met when they were imprisoned at Gila River internment camp in Arizona from 1942 until 1945. After their release from prison they moved to Chicago in search of work, having heard that jobs were better there. My parents married in Chicago in 1946, and I was born there in 1948.

We moved to Los Angeles in 1952 and lived in the Sawtelle/Pico area of West Los Angeles. My dad worked as a bookbinder and later returned to school to become a lithographer. My mom had worked as a beautician

in Chicago and, once we moved to California, she worked in a beauty shop for a while and then she went to work at a local defense plant.

As a kid I took part in Japanese cultural activities, such as Nisei Week in Little Tokyo. We belonged to the local Venice Honganji Buddhist church and went to many of the activities there. My parents are Buddhists and active with the church and we kept a *butsudan*—a Buddhist altar—in our home. We spoke Japanese while growing up, because both my grandparents lived with us and they spoke only Japanese.

There was no military experience in my family prior to my enlisting in the Marines, except for my uncle, who was drafted into the 442nd during World War II and fought in Europe. I was the first member of my family to volunteer for the military.

I was an above-average student through high school and played defensive end in varsity football for three years. There was a handful of Japanese American students at my high school. The composition of students was mostly white, with some blacks and Mexicans, and a small number of Asians.

During my high school years there was a fair amount of conflict at home. My parents were embarrassed by the things I was doing. They wanted me to go in the "right direction," not off to different areas, like the Westside, and get into trouble. I often got grounded and I remember getting really frustrated and mad and angry, and it made me want to do more on the sly. My father would punish me by taking away my driving privileges.

Before graduating from high school in 1966, I had heard about the Marine Corps—that it was a tough unit and had excellent training. By the time I graduated from high school, the war was on and the draft had started. During high school, my plans were to be a dentist or, if that

didn't work out, a pharmacist. In college I tried to be academically strong, but the math and science classes were difficult for me, especially since I was running around partying and goofing off.

Back in junior high, even elementary school, I had this fear of being different from others, growing up in a so-called white neighborhood and being an Asian. If I heard the word "Jap" from somebody, I would get mad and pick a fight. It was always a white person who would say it, so I "got down" on white people. I was usually fighting by myself because I didn't know too many Asians.

As an Asian American growing up in Los Angeles, I thought of myself as a tough kid—and I was pretty tough. I was the smallest guy on the varsity football team, so I had to live up to my image of being tough. I belonged to a small gang called the Satan's Sinners, with seven other Japanese American guys. At Nisei Week in Little Tokyo there was always a fight, at different Buddhist carnivals there were fights; and through them all, we tried to be tough kids. I've heard that in Hawaii they have what's called a *haole* day, a certain day of the year when local Hawaiians go to the beach and beat up all the *haoles* [non-native Hawaiian from the US mainland]. We did that almost every weekend at Hermosa, Manhattan, and Venice beaches. Myself and other members of Satan's Sinners would walk along the boardwalk and if people looked at us funny or stared at us, we would pick a fight with them. We were tough, street-smart kids.

We also tangled with other Japanese gangs. Back then there were the Buddha Bandits from East Los Angeles and other Asian gangs from the Gardena area. We never got along with Gardena people. We always heard that the Gardena kids thought they were better than us because, back then, Gardena was a high-class area. So we would tangle with those kids. When the Satans got together, we popped prescription drugs such

as Seconal and amphetamines called "Bennies," smoked pot, took downers, and beat up on anyone who gave us bad looks. I guess I was a juvenile delinquent; we were just bad and tough guys.

I went to Los Angeles City College after graduating from Venice High School. I wanted to be a dentist or pharmacist so bad and I thought I was studying so hard, but still I was a below-average student. I tried hard to avoid the draft. I stayed in college and hoped the draft board wouldn't pick me because I really wanted to complete college.

I spoke to some of my friends about joining the Marine Corps but not about Vietnam. I wasn't afraid of being drafted, but I was afraid of going to war; I just didn't want to go and fight. I wanted to complete college and become something. I was a tough kid and was used to fighting, but I also wanted to get an education. I didn't talk to my parents about the war in Vietnam before I enlisted.

I got my draft notice in 1967. Boy, I really felt bad. All these years I had studied as hard as I could, and now they wanted to put me in Vietnam. It was a real letdown. Right then and there I started talking to friends and they all told me to try to get out of it. They told me to get notes from my doctors saying that I had an illness. Since I was born with asthma, I thought that might get me out of the draft. I went to my doctor and got a letter about my asthma; I also had a bad knee from playing high-school football and got a letter from my orthopedic doctor. I had also heard that if you had high blood pressure, they wouldn't take you.

On the day of my physical exam, I took all the doctors' letters and a big bottle of *shoyu* [soy sauce], which I drank right before they took my pulse. They kept me six or eight hours, then re-did the tests, and I passed with flying colors. They didn't accept any of the letters from my doctors.

The Marine Corps took everybody at that time in 1967 and 1968. After I finished and had passed my physical, I knew I was going in. When

I got my draft notice I dropped out of college. I got so fed up and felt that there was no use staying in school.

I got together with a couple of my friends from Satan's Sinners and we talked about joining the Marine Corps together. I had to wait four to six months after my physical to get inducted into the Army. Since I had already dropped out of college, I didn't want to have to wait around for that long. Also, I didn't want to go into the Army. I wanted to spend two years and get out and get back into college. That was very important to me. I had heard that time goes by faster because you're constantly doing something in the Marine Corps. The recruiting station was on Pico near Arlington. Since I had been bumming around for a couple of months, not doing all that well in school, my parents thought my joining the Marine Corps was a good idea. They didn't think it was a good idea to go to Vietnam, but they thought being in the military would straighten my ass out.

The DI put me and my friend in front of the platoon and said, "This is what the Viet Cong looks like, with slanted eyes"

Marine Corps Boot Camp was at MCRD [Marine Corps Recruit Depot], San Diego, and lasted thirteen weeks. We arrived in the late afternoon on a Greyhound bus, sixty or seventy of us, and we were all just sitting in the bus when a drill instructor came aboard. There was a Puerto Rican guy sitting in the back of the bus wearing sunglasses and he didn't seem to speak or understand English very well. The DI was a big guy and he told the Puerto Rican guy to take off his sunglasses, saying, "If you don't take 'em off, I'm going to knock 'em off." I was scared and thought to myself, "What am I doing here? Is this really happening?" The Puerto Rican guy just kept smiling. The DI ran to the rear of the bus and took a swing and, BAM!, knocked the sunglasses off his face. I remember looking

back and saw that the guy had blood on his face. The DI said that if we didn't listen and do what he said, this is what would happen to us. I hung my head and felt really scared.

We had three drill instructors in my platoon, two white and one black. After I got the haircut and was issued a uniform, a black drill instructor came up and grabbed my collar, pushing it back and forth, beating on my chest, and yelling into my ear, "YOUR OLD MAN BOMBED PEARL HARBOR, DIDN'T HE!" I remember saying, "No, sir," and he screamed, "YOU'RE CALLING ME A LIAR!" I had a large bruise on my chest after that incident.

My friend and I were the only Asians in our platoon. There was a single American Indian, but all the others were either whites or blacks. We really stood out, being the only Asians in the platoon. Near the end of boot camp, since we were fighting the war in Vietnam, the DI said to our platoon, "You want to see what the enemy looks like?" The DI put me and my friend in front of the platoon and said, "This is what the Viet Cong looks like, with slanted eyes. This is what a gook looks like, and they all dress in black." That was really hard to take. I felt like I wasn't an American. In boot camp the DIs referred to me as a gook and a Jap. When I was in Vietnam, I slugged a Marine sergeant for calling me a gook.

During basic training, I was harassed by a couple of recruits who called me a gook, but I told them that I had been born here. I was mostly friends with Mexicans or blacks during boot camp. The black kids were from Alabama, Tennessee, and other Southern states where there were very few Asians, if any. Everything was new to them. I would talk to the black recruits and let them know where I had been born and raised. We got to become good friends after that.

I was an "expert" at the rifle range and a sharpshooter with a .45 pistol. After finishing basic training I felt ready for Vietnam—lean, mean, and green—I thought I was better than everybody else. When I came home

on leave I went to the old places I had hung out at, and instead of other guys picking fights with me it was the other way around—I'd be picking fights with everybody else. I was satisfied as a Marine coming out of basic training. I liked the status of being number one. It was all brainwashed into your head that the Marine Corps is the best and produces the best, and I believed it. I had a feeling that I would be sent to Vietnam out of boot camp. I had a couple of weeks on leave so I did a lot of celebrating during that time. Coming out of basic training, I thought I was ready mentally for Vietnam. The DIs talked very vaguely about what was going on in Vietnam. They had small pamphlets on areas to be careful in, booby traps, etc. The DIs were all Vietnam vets.

"Ching, Chong, Chinaman, Yellow-Bellied Jap"

We left for Vietnam on a commercial flight out of Edwards Air Force base. We landed at Okinawa first and went through an intensive four to five days of jungle training. We were already Marines and were used to that type of training. We landed late in the day in Danang, a few months after the 1968 Tet Offensive. I was scared because the plane that landed before us was shot at by rockets, and we didn't know whether they had made it or not; I prepared myself for the worst. Before we got off the plane we were told to grab our gear and run to the nearest barracks and wait for orders. It was hot and muggy and there was gunfire as I got off the plane.

I stayed in Danang overnight and was flown to the DMZ on a helicopter. I was with the 12th Marines, 1st Battalion, 3rd Marine Division. My unit was located near the DMZ at Camp Carroll, about ten kilometers south from the DMZ; the rear area was called Dong Ha. The other areas where I was based were LZs [landing zones]: Rock Pile, Mutter's Ridge, and McClintock.

Camp Carroll was a fire base about the size of a Von's Market

(including the parking lot), with 105-howitzers around the perimeter of the camp, together with mortars and a lot of patrols. My specialty was the 105-howitzer. The howitzer requires four guys to operate: two guys to turn it, one to fire, and one to load.

Every day we went on patrols, which consisted of twelve guys randomly picked, walking single file. Patrols took place anytime, day or night, and especially after a firefight. We'd have to go out and check the dead and make sure we'd hit our targets, or just to look over the area. I usually carried an M16 and grenades. Luckily, I was never point man. The patrols weren't well organized. Somedays I would go on five patrols per day—short ones—where we checked the perimeter; on long patrols we would leave the perimeter.

I saw a lot of weird things on patrol. Once we were taking a five-minute smoke break during a patrol and a Marine buddy of mine was leaning up against a bamboo bush. He lit his cigarette and took one puff, when suddenly a green "bamboo viper" snake bit him in the neck. He blew the smoke out and he was dead.

The only other non-combat-related death I experienced happened at Mutter's Ridge while waiting for a helicopter on my way to see a doctor. When the chopper came in, five of us got onboard, but the crew chief told three of us to get off and I was one of those three. The chopper developed engine problems after it took off, and then it went down into a gully. When it got power back and came up again, it got hit by an RPG [rocket-propelled grenade]. Things like that just stay in my head. I think of different holidays and things just pop back into my head from the time in Vietnam and I get flashbacks.

I spent Christmas of 1968 in the Ashau Valley. I was at Camp Carroll for a month and then I went to Mutter's Ridge for a month, and then to McClintock for another month. The most combat I experienced was

halfway between Ashau Valley and Mutter's Ridge, on a hilltop LZ. That's where I experienced my first death. I hadn't experienced death until Vietnam. To have someone die right next to me was very traumatic. I was in a foxhole with a young new Marine, and I explained to him—he had just arrived in Vietnam—never stick your head above the ground; always fan-fire the area first. We were getting hit by mortars. I told him, "Usually, the VC will hit us by rounds of threes. After the third one hits, you stick your machine gun above the ground and fan-fire." I had been told this by more experienced Marines. I guess this new guy got curious. I recall that after the second mortar round hit we were just waiting for the third one, sitting back to back. Finally, the third one hit. I stuck my machine gun above and started fan-firing the area, but before that happened I felt what I thought was wet mud hitting me in the back of my neck and back. After I fan-fired the area, I turned around and looked and saw that half of his head was gone. I was sick for days after that. That was my first experience. I think what happened was that, because the third round had come a little late, he must have either gotten scared or anticipated it in the wrong way. I think he must have stood up and fan-fired the area. You want to stay below the foxhole and stick only your arm up. Being that that was probably his first combat situation, he just freaked out. He was only seventeen or eighteen years old; I was only nineteen at the time.

A new staff sergeant came into our unit, whom we all hated because he had a drill instructor's attitude. He teased me for about a week by grabbing his eyes to make them slanted, and saying, "Ching, Chong, Chinaman, Yellow-Bellied Jap." I couldn't take it anymore, so when I got him alone I slugged him as soon as he said it. I just kept hitting him; I felt like a machine. I just wanted to kill him. A lot of the other guys jumped on him with me because they hated him too, for saying things like that.

They were protecting me. After that happened, I really felt good. I felt like one of them. The sergeant never apologized. He was transferred out, and we never heard of him again.

I had a sense of close camaraderie with the other Marines even though I was the only Asian in my unit; I hung out mostly with the Hispanic and black guys. At McClintock, we slept right on the dirt. If I had known that we were going to stay there longer—say a month or couple of weeks—I'd have gotten ammunition crates, built a hooch, and filled the top with a tarp so that we'd have had some cover. Overall, McClintock was very primitive. We ate C-rations right out of the cans. I was very fortunate because I told my mom to send me canned goods like corned beef and Japanese cookies. She also made great chocolate chip cookies. The food would last only a day or two, because we shared among the other Marines; everybody shared their food. There was some alcohol available at McClintock and other LZs. Our lieutenants would go back and forth to the rear base; if we gave them money to cover the cost of buying a few beers, they would bring them back to the LZ. I don't recall any drug use in my unit where we were stationed.

We had contact with Vietnamese villagers at Camp Carroll, Mc-Clintock, and other LZs when we went on patrols. We would get information from the montagnards—the mountain people—on VC activity, which would allow us to set ambushes and booby traps. We knew the VC were out there, but we didn't know where. On patrols, whoever saw the other first would shoot first. We would walk through both inhabited and deserted villages. Usually there were older people living in the villages, like grandparents, wives, and their kids—but no young guys. It was just like in the movie *Platoon*. We'd try to get information from the villagers, but they didn't want to cooperate—so we'd get brutal, wanting them to talk. There was a lot of slapping and hitting of villagers but I never saw any villagers shot or raped.

When I first got to Vietnam, I remember almost killing the barber.

ark Nakagi, US Army, Tay Ninh, 1969–70. *Mark Nakagi collection*

nother day on patrol. *Mark Nakagi collection*

Just hanging out.
Ross Suehori, US Army, Pleiku, 1966–67.
Ross Suehori collection

Burning villages.
Ross Suehori collection

Wearing Buddhist beads and flashing a peace sign.
Henry Sato, US Army, Camp Enari, 1969–70. *Henry Sato collection*

Posing as the enemy and having fun with the guys.
Joseph Fujimoto, US Navy, Danang, 1966–67. *Joseph Fujimoto collection*

Playing the enemy.
Sam Yorunga, US Army, Ben Hoa, 1969–70. *Sam Yorunga collection*

Getting high with the Royal Thai Marines.
Kyle Miyogi, US Army, Bear Cat, 1968–70. *Kyle Miyogi collection*

"We drank hot tea and smoked before and after dinner while listening to the Doors and Hendrix."
Kyle Miyogi collection

...sing with a captured AK47.
...hn Okabota, US Army, Hue, 1967–68. *John Okabota collection*

Bernie Ashikaga, US Army, Bong Son, 1967–68. *Bernie Ashikaga collection*

Surfing in Vietnam.
Daniel Katsura, US Army, Saigon, 1965–66. *Daniel Katsura collection*

We were going through a village and decided we'd get haircuts. I sat in the chair and I told the barber to trim just a little around the ears. He started cutting and when he was finished and before I knew it—I had my gun right next to my hand, because you don't trust anybody over there— he had grabbed my head and twisted it, cracking my neck. I grabbed the gun and threw it, hitting him right in the chin. Then I pushed him against the wall, but my buddies came rushing in saying, "No, no! It's part of their service." It was a tradition to cut the hair and give a massage. I apologized to the barber. I'll never forget that first haircut.

I probably killed a couple of women during patrols through villages. We would go through a village and we would yell out to the villagers to come out. If none come out, you think it's empty. As you walk through a village that's supposed to be empty and you hear or see something move, you shoot in that area. That's war. During the daytime the villagers were friendly; they gave us food and acted as if they'd do anything for us. Nighttime is when they would change into the black pajamas. It's the enemy. You can't trust anybody.

In terms of my looking Asian, with an American Marine unit, going through these villages, how I was treated had a lot to do with my uniform. If I was wearing regular street clothes, I would be mistaken for a Vietnamese. The uniform and the way I spoke helped to keep me from getting harassed. Some of the villagers would say in Vietnamese, "Who are you?" They wanted to know where I was from because they knew I wasn't Vietnamese. That this was a war against Asians and my being Japanese, I always had the fear of getting shot by an American. If I was with a group of Americans, in uniform, the fear would lessen. But if I was alone walking in the street, I was afraid. There were never any encounters. It happened when other Marines or military didn't know you. They would stare and I would say, "What are you staring at?" When they heard my voice, they would know. It happened with Army guys when we were traveling from one place to another.

I got wounded at LZ McClintock in 1969. We were on a hill cleared of shrubbery and we could see the Viet Cong in the distance. It was after 6 pm and you could still see, but it was getting dark. I remember seeing the VC coming up the hill and we started firing from our perimeter holes. I remember that we were shooting down the hill and at the same time we were requesting artillery support. The next hill over was a Marine mortar unit. We radioed them, gave them directions, and they started firing rounds. We called for a short round and they fired a couple of rounds, but one of the rounds hit us. That's how I got wounded. I didn't know I had gotten hit until the firefight was over. Once I started to relax, I looked down and saw all this blood coming out. I took off my flak jacket, and I was all wet. I had shrapnel all over my chest. Since I was in combat more than eight months, they asked which hospital I wanted to go to. I told them I wanted to go to Japan, so they flew me to Japan for recuperation. I didn't get a Purple Heart because I was wounded by friendly fire. Do you believe that shit! We don't get Purple Hearts for getting hit by friendlies—only enemy fire. Two guys were killed from that same round.

They knew that Agent Orange was a major killer

When I came home in 1969 I had a difficult time adjusting. After I got wounded and was on my way home, I had the feeling I was a hero. I thought to myself, "I fought in the war and I came back in one piece." When I landed at Travis Air Force base I was still in a stretcher. I came back on a C-131 cargo plane with other wounded guys. I remember landing at Travis and being placed in a wheelchair. I remember people standing around the airport yelling, "YOU WOMAN AND CHILD KILLER, YOU DOPE ADDICT." I heard that. From that day on, I didn't want to be associated with Vietnam. I didn't want anything to do with Vietnam or the military because of that bad feeling I got when I came back.

I was sent to a hospital in San Diego and was released in about a week,

back to active duty until I served out my time. I had three or four months remaining in my enlistment contract. I was stationed in Pendleton. They gave me an early out for college. I was also working at a pharmacy so I could study up. It just didn't work out. I went back to college, but all those high hopes that I had of becoming a professional didn't happen.

I went to West Los Angeles College when I came back. I was late for one of my science classes, and I walked into class and may have bumped a chair or something—I made a noise of some kind. The professor, who must have known I was a vet, looked up at me and said something like, "Do you Vietnam vets think we owe you?" I picked up a chair and threw it and walked out. I went back to college but only attended night classes.

By 1969 the anti-war movement was large, as was the counterculture with the hippies, long hair, rock-and-roll, Jimi Hendrix, LSD, and grass everywhere. There were a lot of people who blamed the war on the vets rather than placing the blame on the people who ran the government. That was part of the difficulty I experienced. I was called all those things—things that I wasn't—I didn't kill women and children on a whim; I did it because I had to save my life—it was either me or them. And I didn't do drugs over there. All those accusations upset me.

All the negative attitudes I experienced after returning home were very confusing. It was like, "They owe me something for what I did"—but I never got it. Nowadays I take advantage of the VA [veterans' administration] insurance by going to the VA once or twice a month. I want to get what I didn't get before; I didn't want any part of the VA before. I also didn't want to be known as a veteran. Since 1993 I have had this change in my attitude. I didn't drink when I came back; I didn't grow my hair long. I mainly took narcotics and sedatives. That's what was on the market. I took Quaaludes for a while, which I liked. It was a weekly routine, a weekend job. I hooked up with my old friends from Satan's Sinners when they came

back from Nam. We all partied together. They were supportive of what I had gone through in Vietnam because they had been through similar things. I don't know if they have the type of problems that I have—PTSD [Post-Traumatic Stress Disorder]—for which I collect disability. I've also attended veterans' counseling sessions and different programs for it. The group sessions with all combat veterans were really good. To listen to and talk about combat situations everybody's been through made things a lot easier for me. I could never talk to my parents or any other non-veteran about combat situations, because they couldn't possibly understand what it was like.

I haven't kept in touch with any of the vets I was in Vietnam with. After I was wounded and sent out to a hospital, my unit remained at Camp Carroll and we lost contact. I was in the hospital in Japan for almost three months, returning to the States from there.

I had never heard about Agent Orange when I was in Vietnam. I do remember seeing planes and choppers flying low and spraying stuff, but I didn't know what it was; I don't think any of us knew. I didn't hear about Agent Orange until the 1980s. I remembered going on patrols through defoliated areas. As a matter of fact, when I applied for the Agent Orange reimbursement Dow Chemical sent me a map and instructed me to mark wherever I had been stationed in Vietnam and the dates. They sent the information back to me, saying that I had been exposed, because that's where they were spraying at the times I mentioned. I have copies of that report. Dow Chemical kept that information from the general public. They knew that Agent Orange was a major killer.

If I could go back and do it again, *I wouldn't do it at all*. I would not have gone to Vietnam. If I had had the money and the knowledge, I'd probably

be a Canadian citizen right now. Because I was exposed to Agent Orange and various combat situations, my head is not the same. I only have a quarter of my stomach, because I have an ulcer disease and I've had four stomach surgeries. I'm in a very different place than in 1967. I would advise seventeen- or eighteen-year-old kids to stay in college, try to get into a professional school by any means, because that's what I didn't have. If I'd been in a pharmacy or dentistry school, I would have gotten a deferment.

I'm skeptical toward our government today. Since I came back, I have not registered to vote because I don't feel politicians can do anything for us. Back then, the voting age was twenty-one—which meant you could kill and be killed for your country at the age of eighteen but you weren't old enough to vote. That's stuck in my head ever since. Anything political doesn't affect me. I feel that there is nothing I can do.

CHAPTER SEVEN

LARRY MATSUMOTO

ARMY, 1968–70

BONG SON

I learned early in life what it was like to be disciplined

I was born in 1944 at Heart Mountain, Wyoming, a prison relocation camp for Japanese Americans during World War II. My mother's from Boyle Heights, in East Los Angeles; her family was relocated to Manzanar Relocation Center during the war. My father's family was from Terminal Island and many of them were relocated to Heart Mountain in Wyoming. My parents were married at the time but were separated at camp.

My maternal grandparents were from Kyushu, Japan and my father's family came from a small fishing village on the other side of Hiroshima. Both of my parents' fathers were fishermen. My paternal grandfather started fishing at Terminal Island and my mother's father came to California around 1890, where he jumped ship at the age of fourteen.

Prior to the war my father owned his own fishing boat and worked in San Pedro as a fisherman. The San Pedro guys were very close to the Japanese culture; they spoke Japanese, practiced martial arts at the local Buddhist temple, and were a very tough bunch. Many of them belonged to a group, *yogure*, an early form of Japanese gangsters; that's what I grew

up with. My father was very tough and he taught us to be tough and loyal to the country, and not to say very much.

During World War II their homes and boats were confiscated and the US Navy completely destroyed the whole area near Terminal Island. They demolished all the homes, and the boats were sold to the local Italians and Russians. My uncle got a draft notice while he was imprisoned at Heart Mountain and he said, "Why am I getting drafted in camp?" The government told him that if he didn't enlist in the Army, he would be jailed. He refused to serve in the US Army and he was sent to the Federal penitentiary at Fort Levenworth, Kansas.

A Maryknoll priest my mother knew in Los Angeles contacted my uncle and told him to tell the government that he was Catholic and they would let him out. Instead he told the government he was a Zen Buddhist, not a Catholic, and he was kept in prison for another couple of years. After the war he was released, but he had lost his social security as a result of being incarcerated; he really suffered for having resisted.

The government gave my parents fifty dollars when they were released from camp at the end of the war. We returned to Los Angeles and luckily my mother's family had a house in East Los Angeles. All of the family members stayed with them in a two-bedroom house. I'm told that kids were sprawled all over the floor at night, while others slept in the garage, all the women cooking and washing dishes and clothes. My father had a number of odd jobs. He worked as a gravedigger for a while but eventually he worked for thirty-five years as a truck driver. My mother never worked outside the family; she took care of all the kids. We were a lower-middle, working-class family.

Japanese wasn't spoken in our home because of the discrimination my parents experienced during the war. We never took part in Japanese holidays and we never went to Japantown in Los Angeles. Once, when I was older, I joined the Japanese American Community League (JACL). I was happy that I had joined and I told my parents. My mother said to ask

my dad about the JACL, and he said, "Those are the sons-of-bitches who put us in camp. They were traitors, *inus* [dogs]. They're the ones who collected the addresses of all Japanese Americans from the San Pedro area and handed them to the authorities." My dad was out at sea when the FBI arrested his father, and the authorities already knew which houses to go to. They handcuffed my grandfather and interrogated him.

There was a rift in the Japanese American community resulting from the wartime experience. The Terminal Island group felt that the Japanese American community, instead of being friends to them, had really turned against them. That's part of the reason why my father isolated us from the Japanese American community when we were growing up.

I'm very much like my father—quiet but volatile, at times, with a bad temper. He was very much the disciplinarian. My father required us to be obedient to authority and to him. My mother used to yell at us, but when he yelled we would snap to, like soldiers. I learned early in life what it was like to be disciplined.

In grade school all I saw were Mexican kids and a few black kids. In junior high there was a mixture of kids, some Japanese Americans, a few blacks (which was good, because I got to be friends with them), and Hispanics and some whites. I had friends in all the groups. At Garfield High School I played varsity football. My father, being small and tough, pushed me into sports. Scholastically, I was an average student. I wasn't the stereotypical academic Asian. All the other Asian kids were really "academic Asians." I felt awkward and insecure as a kid.

From the time I was eleven years old, I worked Saturdays gardening for my uncle. I think he took us to work to keep us and his own kids out of trouble. Because my uncle worked for my father on his boat many years ago, my uncle wanted to pay back my dad.

My social life while in high school revolved around football and

gymnastics. I had this blinding tunnel vision: no partying, no drinking, no cruising, no Eastside–Westside gang involvement. I was like a samurai soldier—like my dad. I'm lucky, because it did keep me out of trouble. I was asked to join a Japanese American gang once, one of the Eastside gangs that my cousin was in, but football gave me an excuse to stay out of the gang life. I remember there were many instances of discrimination aimed at Japanese Americans in high school. The Mexicans used to call us "Chinos," meaning Chinese. While some of the Mexican kids were very tolerant and accepting, others were racist.

I didn't really have cultural heroes growing up as a kid, except TV heroes like John Wayne and Gene Autry. I always believed that the good guys were American soldiers, fighting for the country, being loyal and courageous. To this day, I still watch Westerns. These are the romantic heroes that are ingrained in me.

From high school I went to East Los Angeles Community College for two years and was on the football team. I didn't hear about Vietnam during high school. After East Los Angeles College I transferred to Whittier College and majored in biology. I was the first member of my family to go to college. I graduated in 1967 with a degree in biology.

During 1966–67 I started hearing about Vietnam in lectures on campus. Whittier College was a conservative school, so there were no protests on campus while I was there. I only remember a few discussions on the war when I was a student there. I used to go to the dormitories to visit my friends and we talked about Vietnam.

In 1967, during my last semester at Whittier College, I heard Barry Sadler's song, "The Ballad of the Green Berets," and I was mesmerized. I bought the record and listened to it twenty times and decided I wanted to become a Green Beret. My brother had just come back from Vietnam; he had joined the Army right after high school, and he introduced me to a major from a Special Forces group. I wasn't envious of my brother. I had a student 2-S deferment, but I got reclassified 1-A as I approached

the end of my course work at Whittier College. I wrote a letter to the draft board asking them to change it so I could keep going to school, but they refused. I went to the recruiting station in Alhambra and told them I wanted to go into the Army Special Forces as a Green Beret.

We did experiments on dogs

Boot camp was ten weeks at Fort Lewis, Washington. From there I went to Fort San Antonio, Texas for combat medical corps school. I wanted to become a medic because of my background in biology, and I decided that if I enlisted in the Army I wanted to at least learn something. When I was in Texas, a Green Beret recruiter came to talk to our platoon and this was my chance. We had to take a six-hour exam to get into the Special Forces group. The recruiter told us we were accepted but that we had to volunteer for airborne school before going to Green Beret school. I went to Fort Benning, Georgia for airborne training for three weeks in the summer of 1967.

From Fort Benning, Georgia we went to Fort Bragg, North Carolina for three weeks of classroom training. Because of my college degree, I was sent to an Army Special Forces school in Texas for on-the-job medical training. That's where I got a taste of studying under pressure. We were told that if we failed two tests, we would be sent to Vietnam; luckily, I failed only one. The teachers were all working doctors and nurses. After that, I went to a local hospital for an additional seven weeks of on-the-job training and then to a "dog lab" for six weeks, where we did experiments on dogs.

At the dog lab each soldier was allocated a dog. We all named our dogs—I named mine Foxtrot. The dogs were our patients, so every day we took their vital signs (thermometer in the butt), checked respiration, and physical characteristics, wrote reports, practiced giving IVs into their

legs and giving thorazine shots to knock them out. One of our exercises was giving the dogs a shot, shaving their legs, cutting the muscles to expose the vein, and putting a needle in the vein. We practiced this in case an American was shot and we couldn't get to a vein to give a wounded soldier an IV. Everything we practiced in the dog lab was a simulation of how to treat a soldier shot in combat.

One time, we put the dogs under with thorazine shots and ether and laid each down on a stool. A sergeant closed the door in the room and then shot a pistol round into one of the dog's legs. We immediately took the injured dog to surgery, where we cleaned the wound, extracted the bullet, and sutured the wound. A couple of weeks later, we had to amputate one of its legs. This was really weird training!

We had two more weeks of training and lectures involving simulated combat situations with the dogs, and for our final exam we were required to kill our dogs. We injected the dogs with sodium pentothal, put them in plastic bags and sent them to the dump. This part of the training was ugly. In Vietnam I saw one of my friends put into a body bag and I got a flashback about Foxtrot.

I felt pressured because I was the only Asian in the medical training program. Overall, there were few minorities in the group. I felt I had to prove I could be just as good as everyone else in the program. There was discrimination, but it wasn't blatant. When I was in school in Texas, some of the guys in my group were Texans. They said they didn't like a particular Mexican in our group because he was Mexican, and he was like the guy that killed Davy Crockett. Many of the guys wouldn't talk to him, but I did—he was an East Los Angeles boy. That was an ugly experience. I'd seen racism in Los Angeles, but not like that.

After this particular training was finished, all of the units came together

at Fort Bragg, North Carolina and formed Special Forces A-teams consisting of twelve specialists from communications, heavy weapons, light weapons, demolition experts, medics, and officers.

I also volunteered for Army Ranger training, which involved an additional ten weeks in Fort Benning, Georgia. After Ranger training, I went back to Fort Bragg, North Carolina and waited for orders. Our commanding officer put me on detail guarding a little arsenal of M16s and M60 machine guns and other weapons. I did this from 4pm to the next morning, 9am. There was no radio or TV and no one to talk to; it felt like prison. This was when I volunteered for Vietnam. The Green Berets, the young ones who ended up in Vietnam, all had to volunteer in order to go there. I got my orders two weeks later for Vietnam.

Most of my experience in Vietnam was with the montagnards

We left for Vietnam in January 1968 from Washington state. All of us were from different units and no one knew each other. I was so scared! Before we boarded we had to put on our jungle fatigues. I don't recall where we landed in Vietnam. According to my orders my reporting station was Danang, in I Corps. We assembled at a Special Forces group in Danang and went to Nha Trang to train for two weeks in jungle survival techniques. We carried our M16 rifles, practiced radio procedure, conducted small patrols, and ran up and down hills with knapsacks full of sand. Halfway through the first week of survival training, we heard a siren and were told to grab our old M1 carbine rifles—they didn't have enough M16s to go around then. A truck drove by, carrying a dead Viet Cong. Suddenly, it struck me that the enemy had an Asian face. Everyone was using the word gook to refer to the dead Viet Cong. I even saw black guys calling the dead VC a gook. It was a weird experience.

I was never called a gook during my tour of Vietnam. I knew from my

training that everybody else on the team was not an Asian, so I was careful what I did. I knew I couldn't be like everybody else, so I set higher standards for myself. I didn't get drunk like everyone else did, because if I made a mistake I could get kicked out. I had to be a model soldier to be accepted into the team.

After finishing survival training, we were sent back to Danang; from there I was sent to an A-team, A-105, in I Corps, the second closest base to the DMZ, a place called Bong Son. We were located way up in the mountains. From the helicopter looking down, there was a giant brown flowing river and three or four villages. We had village militia supporting us. The camp had been there for three or four years. Seabees and Navy engineers went there and dug bunkers—my room was underground.

A week after I got to Bong Son, I was told that I was the senior medic because of my rank. I told the other medic, "You be the senior medic because you've been here three or four months longer than I have." The medic said, "No, I'm about ready to leave. I've been here ten months." The captain came over and I felt this coldness. He told me, "Sergeant, get ready for a medical mission." He told me I was going with a detachment of Vietnamese to the villages below. I asked if someone could go with me. He refused, saying, "You're going alone." I went to the top sergeant to find out what to take and all he said was that I should know from my training. Depressed, I was walking down the hallway when I saw a black sergeant operating a radio. I asked him what I should do. He took me outside and introduced me to my interpreter and said he was my lifeline. "Respect this guy or you'll die," he said. I shook hands with my interpreter and was introduced to the Vietnamese lieutenant; he told me to get rid of the M1 and get an M16. He gave me a week's worth of rations, which consisted of a bag of green Vietnamese rice. He told me not to think that I was better than the Vietnamese.

Every night at seven o'clock I was supposed to call back to the base with my location, using a secret code. The sergeant taught me how to

code and decode everything. The next day, armed with two bags of medical supplies, I met the lieutenant and we started on our patrol. It took us about forty-five minutes to go down the hill to the villages. We got on a small boat to cross the river and when we arrived at the village, all the villagers were already lined up. I mostly gave out soap. A lot of the kids had scabies on their heads so I gave them injections, and malaria and diarrhea pills. We went from village to village for a week. I called in my position every night at seven o'clock. They told me not to stay at a village more than one day. On the third day, the Viet Cong had entered one of the villages we had just left and killed the villagers.

After a week we went back to the base camp. I was relieved and I never got a word from the captain. He never said, "Good job," or asked, "How did you do?" Unbelievable! That was a standard mission for the Special Forces medics. There were usually two or three Americans to support each other. I don't know why I was sent out alone or why he didn't send me with an experienced guy.

Another incident: the captain called for an airstrike to bomb the villages near us. His intelligence said that there was a buildup of Viet Cong in the area. Anytime we called for a bombing mission, we had to send a patrol out to check for bomb damage assessment [BDA]. The captain sent the black sergeant out alone with a Vietnamese soldier and an interpreter. The other medic, Sanders, and I went to the captain to say that one of us should go too. The captain said no. The next day a group of Vietnamese guys came running up to our camp; they threw down their weapons and food. We said, "Where is the American?" We had heard a distress call coming over the radio. It turned out that the sergeant was running and the VC were after him. We could hear the shooting over the radio. The captain called for a react force of two companies, and a major from that group asked me personally to go out with them. We stayed out for two weeks and we found the sergeant's body lying dead beside the inter-

preter's body. We brought them back. It was a terrible feeling. This black sergeant was on his second tour and had two months to go when the captain sent him out.

Being out so late the night before, I had a headache and slept in late after getting back. The captain found out about this grave transgression and said to me, "Shape up or ship out." I told him I would ship out. He told me to get my butt out on the next helicopter. I packed my gear and went to say goodbye to the sergeant-major, who had been so nice to me. I said, "Sergeant-Major, I just lost a friend out there," and he said to me, "Where do you want to go?" I told him I wanted to go to I Corps.

When I arrived in Danang I was interviewed by a major in Mike Force, C-team. The major was really nice and I had a sense of acceptance and told him I would do my best. I was introduced to the team and immediately went on missions patroling each of the seven A-team sites in our area. The missions lasted for two to three weeks. We had two groups supporting us—a battalion of montagnards and a battalion of Vietnamese. I didn't like the Vietnamese, because they saw me as a weird American. They called me the "short doctor." I liked the montagnards, who were darker, like American Indians.

The montagnards did not get along with the Vietnamese. There was racism there too. We had black guys in the Special Forces and there was tension between the blacks and whites. I don't think I was ever accepted as a soldier there. I was able to go talk to the blacks, and I could talk to the whites too, but I was never totally accepted by either group. I walked a fine line. I was respected by both groups but never accepted. It was better for me because I never developed any attachments. Psychologically, it was easier that way. I was like a half-breed, even though I was a good soldier.

Once we were walking along a ridge on a beautiful, quiet trail. On our left was a lush, green valley. Suddenly we got hit with M70 grenades

and small arms fire, and a couple of my montagnards were wounded. The other A-team thought we were VC because we had all these dark soldiers.

I had contact with South Vietnamese villagers and occasionally we had to kill some of them. That was ugly! Our orders were to search and destroy, and this meant burning their hamlets. Usually the males would flee before we arrived in an area. Our montagnard soldiers would capture the males and take them prisoner or kill them. They did not like the Vietnamese peasants. The montagnards considered themselves the original inhabitants of Vietnam. As a medic I didn't take a direct part in the killings, but I was there with the group. I felt split, being a medic and a soldier, taking part in this genocide. I remember one incident when our commanding officer was screaming at the villagers, telling them to "Get out, get out." A village woman was screaming and yelling as she left the village area. The montagnard commanding officer went into the woman's hut and saw a baby around six months old. We took the baby and adopted it.

The villages were all hand-made and looked prehistoric. We used zippo lighters to burn them. Everything in the village was immaculate, with the rice fields a mere twenty yards away from the huts. There I was, an Asian American soldier, watching montagnards fighting against the Vietnamese. It was a weird situation. Most of my experience in Vietnam was with the montagnards, and I really bonded with them. I learned later on that there was an agreement that the Americans would help the montagnards once the war was over; we never did that. The Americans just let them die.

I didn't think the Vietnamese people wanted us there. We got a double whammy: there were protests in the US against our involvement in Vietnam; and, once we arrived there, the Vietnamese didn't want to have anything to do with us. The Vietnamese troops didn't want to fight, so

the Americans ended up doing 80 percent of the fighting. We engaged in all the hard battles and military missions.

Back then, everybody lied to the American president. After two months in Vietnam, I could tell whether the Vietnamese people wanted to fight or not. The North Vietnamese had a cause and a plan for military victory, and they fought like the Japanese. There were rumors that when Japan was defeated in Vietnam, some of the imperial soldiers remained there, changed their names, became Vietnamese commanders, and trained Ho Chi Minh's forces. I'm not sure, but the VC sappers were sure like Vietnamese kamikazes.

The Vietnam War was about corporate power

I left Vietnam in January of 1970 and landed in Seattle, Washington. I arrived in the States still wearing my jungle fatigues and was given a change of uniform because, we were told, the American people didn't want to see us as jungle soldiers. So we turned in our jungle fatigues. We were given a steak dinner at the airport and told that the American people were grateful for all we had done. I had spent close to two years in Vietnam, and all we got was a steak dinner and a ten-minute speech for all that dedication. I was processed out of the military within a day. I boarded a bus in the morning and nobody was there to greet me or anything. There was complete silence. I took a TWA flight and got back to Los Angeles early in the morning and called my mother.

I was in shock. All the years of intensive training, fighting in Vietnam, and all of a sudden I walk into my parents' home. I took off my uniform when I came home. The first thing my mom gave me to eat was rice. In Vietnam I couldn't eat rice. I felt numb. My parents had a place in Monterey Park and that was where I stayed.

In 1971 I started working toward a teaching credential. I was confused because no one in school asked me any questions about Vietnam.

Everybody was in denial, including the professors. I told people I was a Vietnam veteran, and all I got in return was a cold feeling of rejection. I felt like a Martian or some kind of freak; I felt like I was a black person in Alabama going to an all-white school. No one ever asked why I went to Vietnam. I went because I was taught to do these things—I was taught patriotism. I took a lot of psychology classes from my professors with their PhDs, who never asked a single question about what it was like to be an Asian American and to have fought in Vietnam in an Asian war. As an Asian American soldier in Vietnam, I felt complete isolation. There was no place for me as an American soldier in Vietnam.

When I came home and went to Asian areas and met other Asians involved in community groups, they were all anti-military, anti-American, and anti-war. At that time, I wasn't against the war. I met some members of *Gidra*, but I couldn't get into any of the groups. There was never a confrontation, but it was like being back in the A-team in Vietnam. I felt a response of coldness and even outright rejection because I couldn't buy into the anti-American attitude. Many of the Asian Americans who opposed the war were radical Maoists. Having been raised in a conservative family, I didn't really have a critical attitude toward the United States. I wanted to fight for my country.

My father was bitter about being forced into the camps during World War II, but he still told us to always support our country. My parents never told us not to go to Vietnam and supported us when we volunteered. When I returned home from Vietnam, my parents were my major support group. I didn't get any support from the Japanese American community.

Feeling isolated and numb, I immersed myself in college studies. I majored in Spanish literature with a minor in psychology and started teaching in 1971. All my energy was spent on getting my thoughts away from my psychological problems and into my studies. I became a samurai student. My military training and the sense of isolation I felt helped me

to focus on my studies. I put all my mental energies into my studies. I teach biology now at a local Los Angeles high school.

If I had to do it over again, I would never go to Vietnam. It was all a sham. If I had been a military advisor sent to Vietnam, I could have told them in two months whether the Vietnamese could fight or not. The sham was that the Vietnamese people were never prepared to fight, but the American people were told that they wanted to fight for their democracy. As far as I could see, the Vietnamese people cared only about planting rice and living their lives as farmers. I realized that only after going to Vietnam. Anybody with any intelligence could have written that report.

There was so much corruption in the military. The American soldiers were doing all the fighting while the ARVN were kicking back. The American soldiers hated the South Vietnamese soldiers and called them gooks. Today I'm mistrustful of the American government. I was a hard-core, model soldier during the war. Today my feeling is that our government betrayed us.

The Vietnam War was all about American corporations wanting to develop military weapons for sale. We got into war to sell weapons and billions of dollars of medical supplies. The war had nothing to do with patriotism but everything to do with corporate power. I think that's why Kennedy was killed—because he said he didn't think it was going to work. At that time, I bought into the system.

Because the Vietnam war was about corporate power, let's not get involved in another war like Vietnam again. I'm very cynical today about our government. Our leaders lied to us. Corporations made a profit out of this war.

I have never told any of my thoughts on this subject to my students because I'm afraid they're not intellectually ready to learn this kind of trial. I don't know how they can learn it. Not even the teachers ask me anything. I've never been invited to the history classes. We have about

six or eight Japanese American instructors, and not one of them has ever asked me to talk about the internment camps or Vietnam; they really don't want to talk about either subject.

We got the double whammy, being Asian American. Even though we were taught from our internment camp days to be good soldiers, today I respect the Asian Americans who stayed back and said that the war was a sham, but for some reason I still can't get into that openly. I'm still the model soldier trying to be the "good American." The other side tells me this is wrong, so I feel this conflict. I can't protest, but I want to. It's a very complex feeling. I should protest, but I can't, nor can I be a 100 percent gung-ho soldier again.

CHAPTER EIGHT

LAWRENCE YOSHIDA

ARMY, 1968–70

SAIGON

I ditched school and went surfing

I was born in East Los Angeles in 1950. My parents separated when I was three years old. For most of my life we were a working-class family; my mother was a single parent working for the Retail Clerks' Union. My grandmother, who was an *issei*, first-generation, moved in with us when I was seven years old. I was influenced by my mother's critical awareness of social problems. She was in her early twenties when I was born and my father was in his forties. Being a divorced single parent was hard for my mom, but she always encouraged me to go into sports and the Boy Scouts—even if the added activities added to her workload.

My main interest throughout my high-school years was surfing. I ditched school and went surfing whenever I found the chance to do so. I was the only kid from East Los Angeles interested in surfing—no one in my neighborhood or school surfed. Since I didn't have surfing buddies at school, I went by myself to the beach, hitching rides on weekends out to Redondo Beach, Huntington Beach, Santa Monica, Malibu, and even further north. One of the more positive things about surfing for me was

that I met and made new friends. My surfing also kept me separated from the East Los Angeles cultural scene of gangs and fights all through high school.

Around the same time, I started losing contact with my Japanese American friends in school and in my neighborhood in East LA. Since I was interested in surfing, I listened more to white surf music than the Motown that my Japanese American friends were into. I also dressed differently from my East LA friends.

I had heard about Vietnam by the time I graduated from high school in 1968. At the time, everybody in school was anti-Communist. I remember a history class in which the teacher commented on the war in Vietnam, and from his description it sounded like a small war. When I was in high school I didn't know anyone personally who had gone to Vietnam. I would hear about other people's older brothers or friends who had gone, but nothing else. The worst thing I heard was that it was a really bad war. Looking back, I was naive about what was going down in Vietnam and blindly went into the military when I graduated from high school in 1968.

My mom expected me to go to college when I finished high school. She had worked and saved money for my college education, and when I realized everybody was going to college and I was still working part-time pumping gas for $1.20/hour, I felt like I should be doing more. I started visiting friends at their various campuses, like Trade Tech, East Los Angeles Community College, and UCLA. At home my mom would lecture me about doing something with my life. My uncle was a career Army man who made the Army sound like fun. I thought I'd better get the Army experience behind me—because if I didn't, the draft was going to get me. I thought I could go to college afterward on the GI Bill and get my mom off my back and move out of the house. That was my logic at the time. Because I was under eighteen years of age, my mother had to sign a release for me to join the Army. She signed all the papers for me,

but she was really worried about the war. The recruiter told her she didn't have to worry because, being the only son with no other men in the family, I would be sent to Europe or be stationed stateside. She felt reassured by the recruiter and thought it would "make a man" out of me.

"I'm an American from California"

I was sent to Fort Ord, California for basic training in 1968. I remember being singled out as Asian when other guys in the platoon would say to me stuff like, "Are you a gook? You should be on the other side." I had to keep telling them, "I'm an American from California." The recruits also thought I was a homosexual, since I came from Los Angeles.

I was sent to Fort Wachuka, Arizona for AIT [Advanced Individual Training] as a clerk-typist; when I finished, I got my orders for Vietnam. I felt like I couldn't tell my mom that I was going to Vietnam, since she had believed what the recruiter told her about my being stationed here or in Europe. My mom and my grandmother drove to Arizona looking for me because I hadn't called her about graduating from AIT. She had found out about my orders and said she was going back to talk to that recruiter. As Japanese, we are taught not to make waves and to go with the flow. But my mom wasn't like that. My grandmother was very negative and kept telling me that I was going to die if I went to Vietnam; she gave me a small Buddhist prayer book in a fabric case and prayer beads to take with me. After I had accepted my grandmother's religious gifts, she said that I was going to come back alive.

I was living life to the fullest in Saigon

I returned to Los Angeles for two weeks before going to Vietnam. I stayed home and spent time with my grandmother and my close friends. I left from Travis Air Force Base in July of 1968. I remember the

stewardesses were dressed casually and I thought, "This isn't going to be so bad." We stopped in Okinawa and landed at night in Bien Hoa. The flight captain came on the intercom and said that there was a lot of action going on below, that he was going to turn off the cabin lights, and that we were going to land hard. He said that after the plane was on the ground, the cabin lights would remain dimmed and we should run toward the exit by following colored lights on the ground. I heard guys crying in the plane as it made a drop landing. Stepping out of the plane, I felt the heat and sounds from all over the place; bombs going off and small arms fire. I remember people running in all directions. I ran into a tented area where a group of Vietnamese were squatting very quietly. I was gasping and looking at them, and I thought to myself that they all looked like me. My uncle had told me that when the shooting started, they weren't going to stop to notice that I was an American, so he recommended that I stay in the rear. I wondered to myself then what the other American guys were going to think now about my being Asian.

An Army captain during AIT warned us not to trust the local Vietnamese kids, reinforcing his message by showing us a wound and scar tissue inflicted by a kid on his last tour of Vietnam. It left a big impression on me. In AIT we were taught how to fire the M16 for a quick kill. We had the pop-up targets, which we didn't have in basic. There were pictures of the hats Vietnamese wore in the field. I thought that the Vietnamese were going to look more like Chinese and that I would be able to tell the difference between Chinese and Vietnamese, Japanese and Korean. But I found out quickly, after I saw the huddled group of Vietnamese that first night at Bien Hoa, that I couldn't tell the difference between Asians. This created great distress for me because I realized that if I couldn't tell the difference, then other Americans couldn't either.

*

That first evening in Bien Hoa, the base kept getting hit by mortar rounds. Newly arrived guys were pulled out to walk the perimeter, dig trenches, and do guard duty. During one of the night attacks a young lieutenant, who happened to be from Huntington Beach [about twenty miles south of Los Angeles], came in and said to me, "You're a clerk-typist, right? You want to go to Saigon?" I said, "Yes, sir," and the next morning I got orders for Saigon.

I was in Saigon with the 27th Data Processing Unit, where we coded and sent unclassified and classified field reports, for the entire length of my first tour. I had a security clearance for this job and worked in the same building where General Abrams was located at MACV [Military Assistance Command Vietnam]. Working there about as safe as anyone in Vietnam could get, because this building was a bunker and a maze and impossible to penetrate. My job was like a regular civilian one; I worked from eight in the morning until eight at night with two hours for lunch.

Our primary responsibility was to receive information from the various Corps and to code data into line items, such as kill counts, numbers missing, injured, weapons captured, weapons lost, etc. We coded all of this information for transmission overseas. We also had a hotline to the White House, to CINCPAC [Commander-in-Chief, Pacific], and one to Paris when the peace talks started. I worked with four other enlisted men, opening up the scrambled lines in the morning and closing them at night. I saw the entire Vietnam War operations going on at MACV. In the end, the type of work I did really confused my thinking about the war.

At first, we split up the coding by various Corps, such as I Corps, II Corps, III Corps, and IV Corps. As I started shifting things around and comparing numbers, I began to realize that a lot of people were getting killed. My roommate worked with me. He was coding the information

given to the public by the press in the next room, but my numbers and his numbers were not the same; his had fewer Americans dying and more enemy being killed. I realized then that there was a lot of misinformation being sent out to the public and that eventually this deception would catch up with us.

I was one of the few enlisted men at MACV, and whenever any of the officers or generals went out into the field, they would take one of us with them as a driver and gofer. In this capacity I watched them do body counts; once we flew over an area after a B-52 raid and the devastation was incredible. There were all these plastic bags out there with our guys supposedly counting bodies of enemy killed. But they were merely picking up body fragments—anything to put in the bag—and counting each one as a single kill. An officer told me to remember that the numbers we received at headquarters were already inflated in the field, so reducing those numbers before releasing them to the public was all right. We were told that in the field it wasn't possible to get a full body with all the parts into a body bag. That was their justification for changing the numbers at that other level. The units at the field level got rewards based on kill ratios. I was freaked out when I came back from that first observation. After a while, though, I became numb to it and didn't care about the kill counts. A guy would pass out fifty bags, and if nothing came back he would turn in fifty as the enemy kill count. There was a rumor that the ROK [Republic of Korea] troops threw animal parts into their body bags for kill counts.

I was told by my commanding officer that lying was for the good of the American people because the truth would only fuel the anti-war movement. That was the justification for changing the numbers on the kill counts, and it was accepted by everyone working at MACV. This is what the Pentagon Papers were all about. When Melvin Laird, the secretary of defense, came to Vietnam and visited MACV headquarters, we were told to put all of our papers away in our desks. They gave us other papers to

have out, so that if Laird were to see the numbers it would look pleasing. Once he was gone, we got the all-clear and everything came out of our desks. That was the game played there.

I used to drive a motorcycle from my apartment to MACV headquarters. I lived in an old French apartment in Saigon with a nice patio in the back, five bedrooms, all for one hundred American dollars a month. I had some wild parties there. I became friends with a Vietnamese girl and had her live with me; it's cheaper to live with the whores than to pay for them every night. It cost five dollars to get laid and all-nighters were ten to fifteen dollars; if they were bar girls it could cost up to twenty-five dollars. It was cheaper to have them live with me and my roommate; besides, we provided them with room and food. In the end we got screwed because one tried to steal my camera and another one, before she split, was trying to steal the refrigerator. My live-in girlfriend spoke very little English. Many of the young girls living in Saigon were straight from the farmland, forced into prostitution and trying to get whatever they could, and were out to rip us off.

I went to Bangkok, Thailand a few times for R&R, rest and relaxation. On my first trip I met a Chinese guy whose relatives were in the Chinese crime organization in Bangkok and Saigon. While we were talking, he told me that if I carried a briefcase into Bangkok he would fix me up at a hotel with a girl for the entire week. I agreed, and when I arrived in Bangkok a car was waiting for me at the airport. I handed over the briefcase and was taken to a hotel, where I showered and changed, and then I was taken to a massage parlor, where I was introduced to a girl who had been paid to stay with me for the whole week. The girls were beautiful in Bangkok. The girls at the massage parlor cost thirty-five dollars a night back then. The entire week I was in Bangkok, I had a free hotel room and free girls. I went clubbing and traveled around the city

during the day with my girl and came back to the hotel at night. The Chinese guy whose suitcase I'd carried, and who lived in Saigon, told me to call him anytime I was going to Bangkok. I later found out that I was carrying jewelry in the briefcase.

I developed a lot of good sources for grass in Vietnam. There was a guy from California who could score acid and we also had good connections for opium. Saigon was good mostly for weed and opium, even though the weed quality wasn't very good. In Nha Trang, where I was stationed at the end of my second tour, everything was available—psychedelics, grass, and opium. Most of what I bought there was already rolled and cost a dollar for ten joints. Opium came in a liquid form in a small vial with a dipstick that we brushed onto the joints.

There were good opium dens in Saigon, but my favorite ones were in Nha Trang. It cost five dollars per hit and we could stay there as long as we wanted. The rooms were real dark, with pillows all around, like in a bedroom. The opium was smoked in a water pipe. I remember seeing other American service guys in the dens but, for the most part, the majority were older Vietnamese.

I knew an American GI from Whittier, California who was getting his acid mailed in and selling it for a quarter a hit. He had a lot of different kinds of acid, such as the "Wedge," "Orange Sunshine," "Haight," and "Windowpane." The paper blotter acid always got wet; I liked the little tabs better because they would stay dry in a film canister. Liquid speed was also available, for one to two dollars, and came in small vials that we poured into our soft drinks. In Nha Trang, there were Vietnamese kids with fruit carts who would sell drugs to us. When I was stationed there, we got two-hour lunch breaks, during which I would go to the beach and get stoned. There was one Vietnamese kid who had really good weed and

he'd sell me a large bag and I'd smoke it with my buddies while sitting on the beach.

I don't recall seeing the local Vietnamese smoking weed on an everyday basis. Occasionally I'd see local Vietnamese girls with GIs smoking weed. The "cowboys"—the Vietnamese pimps who sold the girls—would smoke, but it was only for show. From the way they held the joint, it didn't look to me like they were really smokers. I also remember seeing marijuana plants growing out in the fields close to our military compounds.

I had a full-time maid when I lived in Saigon and I bought food right off of the street. My roommate liked Asian food and we ate Japanese food I had the maid prepare. The food was not exactly the same, but the basic thing was the same and it was really inexpensive. Vietnamese food is a lot spicier; they use red peppers in some of their dishes.

In Saigon I had connections with Vietnamese people who owned the local clubs and bars. I would supply them with liquor through military ration cards and bring in bottles of whiskey for all of us to drink for a week at a time. Once we got to trust each other, a bar owner would give me names of contacts in the military exchange from whom I could buy liquor without having my ration card punched. He told me to talk to a particular taxi driver at such-and-such time outside the military exchange and give him a card with his name on it. After a while it was a weekly thing: on Saturday mornings I'd meet the taxi drivers, buy the liquor and cigarettes and whatever, and put it all in the cab, the ration cards untouched. I got repaid by the bar owners with special favors and drinks.

I also got involved in laundering greenback dollars for military currency in Saigon. The usual exchange rate when I was in Saigon was one hundred military dollars, or MPCs, for one hundred piasters. Now, if we had

greenbacks, or American dollars, we'd get at least a 2:1 ratio; after a while, we learned how to get 4:1, or even more, for the greenbacks. I converted the piasters back into MPCs, which was hard to do. We weren't supposed to have any greenbacks in Vietnam. I was supposed to leave Vietnam in September, but instead I stayed an extra month because I had suitcases full of piasters and I didn't know what to do with it all. I used piasters to pay for food or weed, living expenses, women, and so on. I had to convert the piasters into MPCs so I could get it into my checking account and converted into greenbacks once I came home. I was warned that if I sent too many MPCs back home (they knew how much we made), we would be busted. Some guys got real greedy that way.

When I lived in Saigon, I would stay out all night at the bars and clubs because I looked Asian. After work I'd change into civilian clothes; none of the American military police could tell the difference between a Japanese American GI and the local Vietnamese. The nightly curfew in Saigon was ten o'clock for regular military personnel. Officially, we were not allowed to wear civilian clothes into Saigon; on base we could wear civilian clothes but not off base. At that time there were a lot of American civilians working in Saigon and they were out until the early morning hours.

After my first tour was over I wanted to extend it by another six months, because I really liked living in Saigon. I was also sending a lot of money home to my mom. I wanted to stay there because nobody saluted officers and everybody did their own thing. Like they said, "What are they going to do, send me to Nam?"

I really felt that I was living life to the fullest in Saigon. There was always the possibility of death, but that reality faded in the light of doing everything I couldn't do if I was in the States; I drank, did drugs, and had lots and lots of girls. As a kid in high school I had never dated a girl, but in Saigon I was in hog heaven. I thought to myself, "Why give this up now?" Saigon had a great nightlife seven days a week. I usually went back to my apartment around 2am. Later than that got scary because we didn't

know who was out there. The period of 10pm to midnight was nice because the American GIs had all returned to base but the nightclubs were still going strong.

I would rent a board from a local Vietnamese kid and go surfing

When I got my new orders to go to Nha Trang, the officer explained that, because I had been dealing with classified documents, I couldn't return to my old job. I told him nobody had told me that. I was to report to II Corps' MACV headquarters and from there I was to be assigned to a field position. I thought I was going to join some advisory team; instead I was stationed at headquarters. I stayed there six months, then extended again for an additional six months, but got an early out on the second extension.

Once my orders came in for my transfer to Nha Trang, I gave up my apartment and my live-in girlfriend in Saigon. I told my roommate to tell my girlfriend goodbye for me. He came to visit me in Nha Trang and we went to the local opium den and had a good time. He ended up getting married to a girl from Thailand.

At Nha Trang headquarters I was a middle man. When people needed something, I made sure it went to the right person; when the stuff came in, I made sure it went back out to them. This is all paperwork, requisitions, orders, etc. It was a nice, easy job.

The town outside of Nha Trang was off-limits to American GIs—the military was real strict about us not going into town. I still had a good time in the barracks because I could do anything I wanted to. I took a real gamble going into town when my roommate from Saigon visited me and we went to the opium dens. At the base at Nha Trang, up until the 10pm curfew, we could have a girl on base, but they were supposed to be checked out by curfew. The girls would wait in a line outside the gate—sometimes sixty of them lined up—and the guards would check

them in. We learned later to go where the South Vietnamese manned the post, because those girls didn't have to be checked out by 10pm. These were mostly local girls from Nha Trang, sometimes as young as thirteen years old. To them we were gold, because Americans were considered rich. I would pick one from the "herd", or if I wanted more I could have more if I wanted. I mostly got blow jobs from the girls. Having women on base was pretty much ignored by the officers and was considered good for the morale of the men.

There was a warrant officer, a drunk, who told me that when he first came to Vietnam he was anti-drug. But now he admitted, "One thing about all you heads is that at least you show up. I don't go into your barracks at night because I'm afraid, but you get your work done. I know about your afternoons up on the roof and at the beach." We'd go up to the roof on a break and smoke a quick number to mellow out. We scored all the dope on the beach. I surfed regularly at Nha Trang. I had two-hour lunch breaks and since the beach was only a block away, I would rent a board from a local Vietnamese kid and go surfing.

Everybody had good stereo equipment in their rooms because it was cheap at the PX. I had Sansui amps, two Pioneer CS88 speakers, and a reel-to-reel tape deck—it was all good Japanese components. I had one set shipped home and kept another one in my room. The guy from Whittier who supplied the acid was the music guru and introduced me to all the high-end equipment. In our rooms we had parachutes draped across the ceiling and we all had our own mini-refrigerators. On the walls we had black lights and posters. The officers knew, because they did all the inspections. We got stoned in the barracks daily. The heads would drink and smoke on the weekdays, and on the weekends we would drop acid, because acid would keep you up. One of us always stayed straight in case somebody had a bad trip.

*

When I was stationed in Saigon, I heard a lot of lies being told at MACV. In the war room I would hear the frustration expressed by the generals; and when the unilateral cease-fire was announced, they kept their operations going as though they hadn't received the news. I didn't think they informed people in the States about operations in Cambodia. Once in Nha Trang, the base got hit. The local Vietnamese who worked with us didn't come to work because they knew of the coming attack. One of the girls who was a typist for us said that if she told us anything, she would be killed. These people only wanted to grow their crops; they didn't really care about being taught new methods of farming. When GIs acted bad toward the local Vietnamese people, they would tell us, "The VC is better than you!" I think the peasants just wanted to be left alone. Our presence there was a waste.

I was riding on the back of a truck when I first got to Saigon, and I noticed that American GIs would shoot at the Vietnamese villagers who were walking alongside the road, just to scare them. In Nha Trang I rented a boat and one guy who came with us shot at Vietnamese civilians swimming in the water.

In Saigon, whenever a war crime happened there were pictures of the crime scene available at headquarters and we would see them. Talk about man's inhumanity to man. The pictures showed blown-up body parts and fragments and we couldn't tell if it was a female, male, old, baby, or what. The narrative would say something like: a GI got some local girls, got into an argument, took them into a bunker, slammed the door, threw a frag grenade inside, and blew them up. Or a Vietnamese guy was caught stealing something. They would hang him up, cut off his balls, and stick them in his mouth. We would get these line item reports on different incidents, a quick synopsis of search-and-destroy missions, enemy encountered, so many enemy killed, so many friendly killed, the kind of weapon captured or lost. These reports were labeled top secret because the officials didn't want them to get out. The My Lai massacre really

amounted to five hundred killed, but the official report said just over one hundred. Before these photos would come to us, they went to the Corps general and other officers who would decide which to classify and which not to classify. When a specific individual was targeted for charges of a war crime, then it became top secret.

In the field, American commanders didn't want their units to look bad. If they hit the wrong village and killed innocent civilians, they would doctor up the report in the field or at MACV before it went to the States. They might have been checking out the village because Communist activity had been reported, but the report wouldn't show any VC killed.

Phoenix reports came through but didn't get coded. I thought these were flat-out assassinations. The rationale was always, "We're doing it for the good of the country and that's why it's better for the people not to know."

The war was a big mistake, a big mistake

I got out of Vietnam in October of 1970. I landed at Travis Air Force Base and went through debriefing. I remember standing in line thinking I was going to get withdrawal symptoms or start hallucinating. A group of us took a cab to San Francisco airport and we met at the bar to celebrate. The guy at the bar asked for my ID and wouldn't serve me any alcohol because I wasn't old enough—I wasn't twenty-one yet.

My mom and grandmother were happy to see me. I told my mom everything I did in Vietnam. She took it all in and said that she didn't agree with everything that I had done, but she was glad I hadn't got married in Vietnam.

Transition back to stateside was hard because I couldn't relate to the people here. As far as my friends were concerned, they were all into their own worlds; some were still in college or close to graduation. I had

developed a really foul language when I returned home from Vietnam, and I came to realize that I didn't have anything in common with my friends. What I realized in Vietnam was that I didn't really know the people I used to hang with back home.

When I was close to death, as I was in Vietnam, I opened up to people—perhaps the drugs helped—but I got deeper into my own mind. In Vietnam we philosophized a lot, which I had never done before. When I came home, my mom knew I was ready to go to college.

I got home in October but school didn't start until January, so I worked at a nursing home until school started. I was able to communicate with the senior citizens and that really helped me come back to civilization. I got to be good friends with the cook at the nursing home, and he told me, "You had the filthiest mouth when you first came here, but you worked hard, and I figured these old people wouldn't understand anyway. I knew you were a good person deep down, so I never complained."

I started school at a local junior college. There were anti-war groups active on campus and I joined the Vietnam Veterans Against the War (VVAW). If anybody had the right to say anything against the war, it was the veterans. Besides, I could relate to the other vets. What hurt me was that the leaders of the VVAW didn't ask me for any input. We would march, but we didn't talk before or after we marched. It was almost like being in the Army again, where I was taking instructions. I thought by sheer numbers maybe we were saying something. By 1971 the war was starting to wind down, and even in Vietnam people were saying the war was ending. We had the attitude, "I'll believe it when I see it."

I went to California State College at Fullerton for a year and a half, but I didn't relate well to the students there. Once I came back from Vietnam, I never cut my hair. I started coming back home to East Los Angeles on weekends and hanging with one guy I had gone to high school

with. He told me where the dances were happening and that was when I met my wife.

I think the war really hurt this country and really hurt the Vietnamese people. The aftermath from a B-52 strike and napalm attacks destroyed what was once a beautiful country. We really messed it up over there. When I first went into the Army I thought, "We've got to support our country and do the right thing"—but this war was terribly wrong. It's sad to say it, but the war was a big mistake, a big mistake.

As I was so young at the time, the war confused me and I became really hardened. When I came back and was trying to readjust to American society, I realized that what we were doing in Vietnam was wrong. My mom didn't want me to say anything negative about our government or about the war, but when I came back on leave I tried to explain some of this to her. Her response was, "It was for your country. You have to trust the government," and so I tried to accept it.

I've told my son that if our borders are attacked, I think we should defend our country. I don't think we should be in Iraq—because it's all about oil, titanium, and natural gas. When it comes time to make that decision, my son has to do it on his own. He told me once that he feels that because I was in Vietnam, he is obligated to do the same. I told him, "No, it's up to you to do what you want. If you want to go to Canada, I'll buy you the ticket to get out of this country."

CHAPTER NINE

KYLE MIYOGI

ARMY, 1968-70

BEAR CAT

I never thought of avoiding the draft

My parents were born in California and returned to Japan for schooling before the war. My dad returned to Monterey and worked as a fisherman before he and my mom were relocated to Poston, Arizona during the war. They didn't talk to me about their imprisonment experience when I was growing up. I guess that's part of the Japanese culture.

I was born in Monterey, California in 1948 and moved to Long Beach in 1952. My dad worked as a fisherman and my mom worked as a seamstress. I was raised by my grandmother, who lived with us until I was about twelve years old when she returned to Japan. My family were Buddhist but I attended a Presbyterian church until I was twelve, after which I began attending a local Buddhist church. When I was in Vietnam, I carried a small piece of paper in a plastic folder that the reverend had given me for good luck. I didn't wear it but kept it in my footlocker. He had written in Japanese, which I can't read, something like, "Good luck and happy return." It got pretty ragged over time in my duffle bag.

I was more of a social and academic kid in high school, with a 4.0

grade point average. The stereotype of the Asian family where education represents the springboard to a good job, a good job means acceptance and a positive image within the community, and how all of this reflects on the family—that was stressed to me as a kid. I was a good student but didn't consider myself a bookworm type.

I also became a rowdy kid while I was in junior high school. Boys' hairstyles were a little different at the time; there was a style called the "ski-jump" where the hair was flat on top, and on an angle and longer on one side, combed back. I don't know if that was an expression of rebellion—maybe people did think I was studious, a bookworm, maybe not a nerd, and I felt pressure from others because I was getting good grades. I was showing them that I was cool. I wore long black pants, jeans-type, baggy; pendleton shirts—not too different from what urban gangs are wearing nowadays, though I wasn't in a gang. My high school in Long Beach was 50 percent black, 30 percent white, and 20 percent Asian.

I hadn't heard about Vietnam in high school. At home, my folks didn't talk about what was going on in the world or outside our community. As I look back, I attribute that to a communication gap. They were able to speak English but not for heavy conversation, and I didn't speak Japanese or understand it enough for them to have conversations with me. Now that we've gotten older, we have conversations in English. To be frank, it didn't really dawn on me what Vietnam was about even after I got drafted. It started dawning on me after I got there. I knew there was a war there, but I couldn't relate to it, living in Long Beach. I also didn't watch much of it on TV. As a kid I was into other things; music, a little bit of drugs—marijuana, hash, and hash oil. I smoked mostly with my Japanese American friends. My hair was long when I got out of high school and got a lot longer when I returned home from Vietnam.

When I got my orders to go to Vietnam I thought that was okay, but my mom and dad were nervous. My older brother was in the Army 82nd

Airborne in 1964 but didn't go to Vietnam; instead he was sent to the Dominican Republic when President Johnson ordered US troops there.

I graduated from high school in 1966 and got drafted in March of 1968. During the intervening time, I really rebelled. I was a long-hair, rebelling against the establishment. I could have gotten into a university but decided to go to a local community college—but then rarely went to class. My grade point average went from 3.9 to 1.5. I attended the pool halls more than class and lost my 2-S student deferment. Before the second semester ended, I had been drafted.

By this time, I had heard about Vietnam but I still didn't pay much attention to it. I wasn't aware of anti-war protest because I lived in my own little world. I wasn't even aware of the anti-war sentiment until I got home from Vietnam. I was more interested in myself during that time. Based on that mentality, I didn't really care what was going on. At the community college there were no anti-war activities. I saw more of the anti-war movement after I got drafted. That was when my brother-in-law and other friends began getting involved in anti-war and Asian studies. I was drafted right after the 1968 Tet Offensive.

I remember getting my draft notice and saying to myself, "Fuck, I have to go into the Army and they're gonna cut my hair!" I wasn't looking forward to the discipline of basic training, since I was out of shape and weighed the most I've ever weighed. It was going to be a major lifestyle change. Actually, basic training was the best thing that ever happened to me. Some of my friends got drafted around the same time and others kept their 2-S deferment. I never thought of avoiding the draft. As I got older, at different times in my life I have wondered: if I had known more about the Vietnam War and what a waste it was, would I have opted to go to Canada? At the time, because of where I was at in my head, I didn't consider it. My parents were very disappointed, first off because I lost my 2-S deferment and hadn't done well in school. Even though I didn't think they were aware of global situations, because we didn't talk about it, they

were aware of the Vietnam War and the fact that kids were being sent over there.

"Niggers, don't be caught after sundown"

I went to Fort Ord, California for basic training. There were a couple of Asian Americans in my platoon but most were white, some were Hispanic, and there were a few blacks. The physical training was tough for me, being out of shape, and I barely passed the physical part and felt that I had embarrassed myself.

I went to Fort Gordon, Georgia for AIT [Advanced Individual Training] and was there for eleven weeks at radio school, being trained to become a radio teletype operator, an RTO. I don't have too many fond memories of Georgia. The second or third week there, I went into the city of Augusta with three friends—one Hispanic, one black, and one white. As we were driving into the city, I saw a sign on the road that read, "Niggers, don't be caught after sundown." Coming from Los Angeles and having gone to school with blacks and Hispanics, I said, "What is this?" The black guy in the car with us said that this was the Southern mentality. We went to different stores and I could sense the prejudice. I felt that there was prejudice for all of us: I was Asian, my friends were Hispanic, black, and white. I tried to forget that experience, but every time I think of Fort Gordon, Georgia and the South, that experience pops into my mind. I still carry that baggage, and I really have no desire to go to the South. That was the first time since growing up in Los Angeles and being called a Jap as a kid that I had experienced racial prejudice. The black guy was from Alabama and he told us that's the way it was and not to let it bother us. After that experience, I stayed on the base every weekend.

I'm feeling like, well here I am, in the Army and serving our country, because one way of showing that I'm an American and that I care about my country is to be in the service. After my experience in Augusta,

Georgia, I'm thinking to myself, "I'm defending these people?" Now and then, growing up, some people have called me a Jap and it hurts even though I'm not from Japan. Even today, though I know I'm a Japanese American, I still sense people are looking at me and thinking I'm not as American as somebody else because of my Japanese ancestry. In that situation in Augusta, where it was so overt, I felt insecure and unsafe. I thought, "How could they treat us that way when they don't even know us?"

Getting high was a social affair in the Thai barracks

I arrived in Vietnam in late 1968. We flew out of Fort Lewis, Washington, stopped briefly in Anchorage, Alaska, and landed in Vietnam after a twenty-two-hour flight. All the drinks and meals were free on our flight. When we landed in Vietnam and the door opened, everybody just about died from the heat and humidity. After we landed in Cam Ranh Bay we boarded a Chinook helicopter for Ankhe, where I stayed for three months with the Army 1st Air Cavalry.

I was in Ankhe during the rainy season, living in tent city with just a duffle bag. Everything was drenched from the rain. I heard in-coming artillery rounds and rockets daily. My job assignment was radio contact with the choppers. After three months in Ankhe the entire 1st Air Cavalry was relocated to III Corps at Bear Cat for the duration of my tour. Bear Cat was ten miles outside of Long Bien and about an hour from Saigon.

There were Thai and Korean soldiers at Bear Cat. The Korean and Thai infantry would be choppered out of Bear Cat for patrols, or they would go out on foot. The thing I found out about Vietnam very quickly was that there was no front line. It wasn't like a traditional war. The rumor was that some of the local Vietnamese working inside the military compound could be VC. Bear Cat came under mortar and rocket attack at least once or twice a week. Once a 105mm rocket hit a hooch next to

me at around three o'clock in the morning. Fortunately, I heard the round coming in and dove underneath my bunk. The blast killed six people in the US sector, but no one in our hooch got hurt. Again, I started realizing that you don't have to be a grunt to get killed in Vietnam.

I didn't have much in common with the Korean Marines. The ones I did meet knew I was Japanese, and I think there was still a little stigma there from them, even though I was Japanese American. I didn't have any hassles, but not very much warmth either.

The Thai soldiers, on the other hand, were very friendly and they treated me like a brother. I spent more free time in the Thai barracks than in the US barracks. I ate hot, spicy Thai food with them and smoked a lot of good Thai sticks in their compound. The Thai infantry guys would go home to Thailand on leave and come back with duffle bags full of strong Thai sticks and Thai weed. Thai sticks were compressed, oily to the touch, a dark green color, and looked like a solid piece of weed compressed against a stick. We used bongs made out of bamboo to smoke the sticks. We also smoked opium in the Thai barracks. The opium came in the form of a gluey black ball; we'd pinch a little bit off, put it in a glass tube, and light it and smoke it or mix it with the Thai sticks and smoke it.

Getting high was a social affair in the Thai barracks. We drank hot tea and smoked before and after dinner while listening to the Doors and Hendrix. After the bong got passed around, I often became incapacitated. I had to walk close to a quarter of a mile to the American barracks and sometimes it was an interesting walk back through the pitch black night.

The Thai Marines would go out into the field for two or three weeks

and come back to the barracks for maybe a week. They came back with necklaces made out of shriveled-up ears as war souvenirs.

There was a village outside of the compound at Bear Cat and some of the Vietnamese people who worked on the military compound—the hooch maids and others—lived there. A couple of times I drove to the village with a friend who worked in the mess hall, and we took C-rations and gave them to the villagers.

Most of the hooch maids, of all ages, were available for sex; they cleaned the hooch and serviced the guys. We paid them twenty dollars a month for cleaning the hooch and five dollars for other activities. To be truthful, there was nothing to spend money on. The barracks were open, with ponchos strung up to provide some privacy between the bunks, and there would be other guys there, but we'd just get it on with the hooch maids anyway. Not all the maids were available for sex, though the younger ones were. We all knew which ones to approach. They cleaned one hooch but would have sex in any of them. Some of them were picky in that if they didn't like you, they told you to ask another maid. I had one maid that I saw frequently but I had most of my money sent home. While I was stationed at Bear Cat, I got to know some of the young hooch maids—they were just young teenagers—and I would talk to them and ask them what it was like living in Vietnam. They said they were used to it because there was always some other country occupying Vietnam—France, Japan, and now America—and this had become a way of life for them.

Some of the discrimination I experienced from other American troops was in jest, like when guys called me a gook—which they also called the Vietnamese. A guy from Mississippi said to me, a month after he arrived at Bear Cat, "You're just another goddamn gook. You're all the same."

Later we became good friends. I asked him, "Haven't you talked to Asians that you thought were okay guys or girls?" He replied, saying, "No," and that this was the first time he had ever met an Asian except for what he had read in books and seen on TV. Later he told me, "You're just like me. I would have never guessed you gooks were just like us."

I did walk away from there a fuller human being

When I returned home from Vietnam, I started hearing more about the anti-war protests and that's when I started wondering if I should have gone to Vietnam. I started to feel guilty, once I learned what the real issues were. After my return I was involved in supporting the anti-war movement. I began to realize that we should not have gone into Vietnam. On the other hand, I was confused because I had been there, but I didn't want to say I'd been there. Most of my friends were against the war in Vietnam and involved in the Asian movement. I think it was a matter of maturing and having the time to reflect that brought me to the anti-war side.

I consider myself a vet who came home and participated on the periphery of the anti-war movement and within the Asian American movement. When I returned from Vietnam, I started to hear about the war from a very different perspective. The crucial point for me was getting to meet Vietnamese people while I was in Vietnam and finding out that they were human beings who felt caught between two opposing powers, while they were simply trying to survive. I was sensing that they were tired of all the foreign countries and wanted them out so that their destiny could be decided by themselves.

I thought it was unfair that the Vietnamese were treated so badly by the GIs. I didn't feel we were making anything better for them. Before I went to Vietnam and met, talked, and lived with the Vietnamese, I really didn't give much thought to the Vietnamese people at all. They weren't a part of my day-to-day life. I felt that I had a relationship to them, being

Asian. Seeing how they were being treated, at times I related that to how, on a smaller scale, I was treated here, where not only was I told I was different in terms of my looks, but the implication was that I wasn't as good as "they" were. So I guess I got a sense of sympathy for the Vietnamese while I was there. I think they felt more comfortable with me, partly because I was Asian and partly, hopefully, because I treated them with respect. Maybe they related to both. I definitely treated the ones I came into contact with, with respect. I never forced myself on anybody.

I did walk away from there a fuller human being. I didn't have to kill; I definitely would not like to have to carry around a memory of that. There was a lot of confusion for vets coming back—unlike for the guys coming back from World War II—where you didn't want anybody to know you had been to Vietnam. I dealt with the confusion of Vietnam by using drugs for a couple of years. I had a lot of time to think while I was in Vietnam, and I realized I was messing up. I was able to focus more on what I wanted to do when I got back home as far as going back to school. I went back to Long Beach City College for a year and transferred to Woodbury University, where I finished my degree in accounting in 1971.

CHAPTER TEN

MELVIN WADACHI

ARMY, 1969–70

PHU LOI

I never really felt fully accepted by Japanese American kids

I was born in Hawaii, in a sugarcane plantation town called Paauilo on the eastern coast of the Big Island, in 1946. My dad died when I was a year old, and my mother remarried when I was three. My stepfather continued to work on the sugarcane plantation; he also punched cows on the Kukia Ranch in the mountains, sold sewing machines, and worked as an auto mechanic for a while.

When I was ten the entire family moved to Los Angeles because my stepdad got a job in the aircraft industry. We lived for about four or five months in Silverlake, and then my stepdad bought a house in Culver City. There were large Japanese American and Filipino communities there, though it was still predominantly white. I graduated from Venice High School in 1965.

I'm *yonsei*, fourth-generation, and my mother was *sansei*, third-generation; she didn't speak much Japanese. My stepfather was what they called a *yogure*, a tough guy. He didn't hang with Buddha-heads, but instead he

hung with Hawaiians and Filipinos. My family was definitely working-class. My father operated a garage for a while and also worked as an assembly worker in the aircraft industry. Later he bought a gas station and then became a welder with a shop in Venice.

Up through high school I began to break away from the Asian American community. I never really felt fully accepted by Japanese American kids, because my family was from Hawaii; some of them used to make fun of me for being Hawaiian, especially the way I talked, and treated me differently from other kids. The fact that my folks were not active in the local Buddhist church or the community center and didn't make me go to Japanese school added to that gap. We were not estranged or alienated, but the tie wasn't as strong as among some of the others. Among the Japanese American kids I went to school with, I'd say most were from working-class families. Most of the Buddha-head adults were gardeners, but there were some automotive mechanics, a few bureaucrats, and one or two wealthy ones.

Academically, I got As and Bs. Education was generally stressed by my family, though I don't recall them taking extra effort to stress it. In high school I was active in sports; I was captain of the gymnastics team, and that was part of my moving away from my Buddha-head friends. I lettered for four years and went for All City, took fourth on the rings, and was president of the Lettermen Club. I had a 1955 Chevy Belair in high school, a two-door, fire-engine red, dual Carter AFB quads, Corvette cam 327, M & 8 slicks, 4 x 11 rear, bucket seats, Tijuana upholstery, black interior, and a stereo. I belonged to a car club called the Escorts and we cruised Sepulveda boulevard, from West Los Angeles to Culver City, and Van Nuys boulevard in the San Fernando Valley, and from Slauson to Crenshaw in mid-city Los Angeles.

I hung out mostly with guys from the Escorts, composed of whites, Hispanics, and about three or four Buddha-heads. I never got into a fight, but there were stare-downs and all that. We used to come down to

Crenshaw to Holiday Bowl where the Algonquins and Conquistadors would hang out. We also went to Roger Young Park and Women Center dances where other Buddha-heads hung out. I surfed some at the beaches of Santa Monica, Sunset, and Malibu.

I didn't do any drugs in high school. Acid came around after high school, more like 1966, although it was available earlier. Timothy Leary was experimenting, as was the Army in the forties and fifties, but it wasn't out on the street until probably 1966. In those years, people were too scared to bring drugs to school, but they would buy them and use them on the weekends or at night.

I had heard about Vietnam just in passing on TV. Around 1965, my senior year, I recall one demonstration with pickets, involving maybe about ten or fifteen people in front of the high school protesting the war. There was a cafe on Venice Beach called the Gas House; it was painted all black and was a hang-out for beatniks, who would hang out on the lawn in front of the cafe, playing bongo drums and congas. That cafe had the most concentrated population of the avant garde intellectual left during that time. In the early part of the war, when America was just beginning to get into Vietnam, people like Allen Ginsberg began to speak out about the war.

By the time I was graduated from high school, I was a conformist Buddha-head kid—quiet, getting good grades, but curious and intrigued. I went to UCLA in the fall of 1965 and got kicked out in January of 1966. I discovered the pool hall and hated eight o'clock classes—and ended up transferring to Santa Monica City College. After that jarring experience, I hit the books and got As and Bs. That event—that one semester—fucked me with the draft board. Because I had flunked out for that one semester, with less than a 2.0 average, I was draftable. My student deferment was in question; and once I got on the shit list, it

wasn't easy to get off. They regularly called me and I regularly had to show them my transcripts and prove that I had maintained a 2.0 average. I was under tremendous stress to avoid the draft. By 1966, I was learning more and more about Vietnam; that it was an illegal war, that it was a racist war, and that it was to a degree an "opium war."

I read a book titled *The Opium Trail*, about how the Guonmingdong Army in China was driven into Southeast Asia and set up a base in the iron triangle mountains of Burma, Laos, and Cambodia, controlling all the opium production there. It was in the interest of American policy— and the CIA in particular—not to allow Burma, Laos, and Cambodia to dislodge the Guonmingdong. The CIA therefore assisted them in shipping the opium out of the area. When I was in south China, I saw this. I actually saw Air America ships with opium bundles refueling and taking off. In retrospect, it's convenient for me to declare the war illegal when I was under the draft. But the point is, regardless of the motivation, I was opposed to the war. I finished Santa Monica City College in the fall of 1967 and began classes at California State University, at Northridge. By the spring and summer of 1968, I was attending anti-war demonstrations.

The other side of life for me by 1968 was drugs. I smoked grass, dropped reds, and eventually went to speed and heroin. I also did some "Strawberry Sunshine" and "Purple Haze" along the way. I remember walking into the cafeteria at Santa Monica City College and seeing a Buddha-head guy sitting at a table with a shoebox full of vials containing purple liquid and a sign in front saying, "LSD—five dollars." It was not illegal at the time. The year of 1968 marked my entrance into the counterculture. I started growing my hair long then. I did LSD a dozen times over a two- or three-year period. I don't recall having a thoroughly blissful acid experience. It was always marked by some fear and depression. There were fun times and dark times.

LSD accelerated my intellectual understanding of the issues of the day. I think acid led me to my more active pursuit of issues important to me:

reassessing American capitalist society; reassessing goals and dreams that I assumed everybody held; reassessing my values; reassessing the contradictions in society; taking a look at things such as the clothes I wore, the length of my hair, the kinds of leisure activities I involved myself in; reassessing the kinds of contradictions that occur within a family and community—this became paramount. LSD accelerated my pursuit of honesty and clarity and had a profound impact on my consciousness. I studied philosophy, political economy, Marxism, and religious studies, and read Kahlil Gibran. I was a pre-dental major before acid, and then I switched to philosophy after acid.

I started at California State College at Northridge in the fall of 1967. The draft board was still on my case, although I was still doing all right in school. Toward the end of the spring semester I was burnt out with school; I was angry and I was doing a lot of dope. I was under a lot of stress, and my grades slipped, although they were above 2.0. I found school to be irrelevant. In the summer of 1968 I did my mandatory hippie tour of San Francisco—spent the summer there, living on the street, selling *The Berkeley Barb*, living in somebody's cellar with a few friends from Los Angeles. By this time there was a circle of us who were Buddha-heads, hippie, dope-fiend, drop-out types. Coming back after the summer, I enrolled in school. After the fall semester, I said, "Fuck it," and just dropped out. From around December 1968 to July 1969 I lost my 2-S deferment, and I was heavily into heroin and speed. I was working and maintaining an apartment in Venice, but it was a pretty crazy period.

I was so fucked up during this period. All that I had learned or felt in terms of my philosophy was overshadowed by the drug lifestyle. By 1969 I was a working addict. I kept paying my bills and maintained my fifty-dollar-a-month apartment, but it was almost a daily thing of having to

score and being paranoid of cops. By the spring of 1969 I stopped using heroin and was using methadrine. I was on about a forty-five-day run when I got the draft notice. My only two options were to flee to Canada or go into the military. I was so paranoid and so zonked out, seeing some of the shit that I saw with some of my friends at that time, that leaving for Canada was not viable. I was scared and thought I was going to die. With all of the chaos, I felt that if I didn't report to the induction center and just stayed with those people I was hanging with and continued to do what I was doing, I would probably die. So to the draft board I said, "Take me, I'm yours." I don't know what it is they looked at; I don't know if they took my blood pressure or anything like that—but whatever they did, I got in.

"You've got my body, take care of it: I want it back in a year"

I slept a lot in basic training. The drill instructors made us run, do exercise, and eat. My attitude was, "You've got my body, take care of it: I want it back in a year." On day one in basic, in my still highly paranoid state, I signed up for another year to get my choice of school. Otherwise the Army was going to put me where they needed me, and I knew what they needed—grunts. There were about a dozen guys, and we went into the next room and looked down the list of schools. I was so scared. I thought, "I was an auto mechanic before going in," so I looked down the list and saw helicopter mechanic—that seemed like a step up. I said, "I'll take that." What they didn't tell me was that the crew chief flies in the ship, sitting there waiting for something to fix in the helicopter, but also acts as a door gunner.

After finishing basic at Fort Ord, California I went to Fort Hunter in Alabama—altogether, two months of boot camp and two months of

helicopter school. Then I went home on leave just before Christmas, reporting back to Fort Lewis, Washington, from where I was sent to Vietnam.

I was just a dope fiend

We landed at Cam Rahn Bay during the night. When the door was opened, all the heat and humidity hit me. I spent about a week in three different transit camps before making it out to my unit in Phu Loi, about fifty clicks northwest of Saigon. I stayed there about three months with the 16th Air Cavalry, First Infantry. I had kicked my addiction in boot camp, but once I got to Phu Loi I started smoking dope again. All we did was: get up, go to work in the hangar, go back to the barracks, and then pull perimeter guard. Vietnam had a whole variety of new drugs. They had all this exotic grass—Cambodian red, Thai sticks—and it was really fun to do.

I bought grass from the hooch maids, the Vietnamese girls who cleaned our rooms. The barracks or hooches were two-story wooden structures with slats on the sides and screens so that the air flows right through. Basically, everybody bunked out in these barracks. We hired Vietnamese girls—some were adult women—and they washed our fatigues, shined our boots, swept and mopped the floors, and traded dope for greenbacks, cigarettes, or piasters—Vietnamese money. We told them what drugs we wanted and the next day they would come back with the stuff.

Grass came in packages of cigarettes that had been opened and the tobacco taken out and the dope put in. There was one sergeant at the motor pool who used to buy a .50 caliber ammo can full of it. I don't know how many pounds there were, but it was all clean stuff, and we could get it any way we wanted. One of the cottage industries in the village was rolling joints; old ladies would be sitting there with a big basket of grass and a bunch of paper and rolling joints all day long. They

would take a piece of bamboo that's cut round, like *hashi* [chopsticks], split one end, cut what looks like a piece of brown paper bag and stick it in the slit, and then put a rubber band on top. It's essentially a flag. They put the paper on the flag, put grass on it, and rolled it. They could roll a joint in five seconds. It was really inventive and I was impressed. I brought one back and I still have it.

I did uppers and downers that were from French pharmaceutical companies. There were small vials of speed that we just snapped at the neck to open, and out would flow the liquid speed. We'd take a vial, pop off the neck, and dump 2cc into a can of soda. France still had commerce and diplomatic relations with Vietnam during that time. Actually, the French stayed in Vietnam the entire time we were fighting the war. The French army had left, but French businesses, residents, plantation homes, and hotels were still there. Essentially, the French got a new army to take care of their business. The US Army moved in when the Vietnamese kicked out the French Army. I'm not saying that the French elite, by themselves, conspired to get the US to send troops over, but they certainly supported our stepping in to try to keep the North and South separated and Diem in power.

Marijuana was big business in Vietnam. Many of the peasants would have had a hard time surviving if they weren't involved in the grass trade. The grass in Southeast Asia is legendary. I wonder, now that the United States has reopened diplomatic trade and relations with Vietnam, if we're going to see Cambodian red and shit like that coming into the States. There are Thai sticks here, but we haven't seen Vietnamese or Cambodian grass in this country yet.

Initially, I'd take a couple tokes of the local grass and have to put the joint out because I'd have trouble walking and talking. Over time I built up a tolerance, but it was extremely strong grass. We also did a lot of liquid opium. Like cocaine, liquid opium came in a little bottle with a plastic top. We dipped our cigarettes in the liquid opium and smoked it.

Liquid opium looked like *shoyu*, [soy sauce] and even smelled like it, but it didn't taste like *shoyu*. Two drops of liquid opium would be equivalent to about a spoon of heroin. We'd take two drops of opium, add water, cook it, and then shoot up.

The first time I hit an opium den was in Vung Tau, a port and resort town, down river from Saigon. When I became a helicopter inspector, I ordered replacement parts from the depot in Vung Tau. If I worked it right, I could get the company commander to approve a trip to Vung Tau to make sure we got the right parts. About once a month or more, I'd go there and party. Vung Tau was a fun place, largely French, and a huge depot area. I'd get one of the warrant officers to fly with me in one of the choppers. We'd spend the night, party, get the part the next day, and fly back. There was an opium den in Vung Tau, but there were several opium dens in Canto, where I was later stationed.

The opium den was nothing more than a hooch with mats, a tray with the opium pipe, and a lamp. In Vung Tau there were two mats for each tray. Going into the den, I'd lie down and the owner would lie down next to me. A piece of solid opium is about a quarter of an inch long. The owner would heat it over the fire to soften it and roll it around the top of the pipe block to shape it, so that it was the shape and size of the hole. When it was the right size, he'd stick it in the hole and make sure that the pin opened up a hole clear to the bottom. So what you have is a block of wood with a hole in it that's lined with opium. Holding the pipe upside down over the lamp causes the opium to start to burn. The owner would do all the work. You have to take all of that bowl in one draw; otherwise the shit gets all fucked up in there. If you leave opium in the pipe it will plug it up because it's soft. Then the owner has to spend more time cleaning the shit out. The first time I did it, the guy started yelling at me, and I didn't know what the hell he was talking about until somebody explained that I had plugged up the pipe.

The opium smoke was really smoky; it's like inhaling cigar smoke. The

smoke is heavy, but you're so fucked up in a few seconds that you don't really notice. It goes straight into the bloodstream from the lungs. You have to take a slow, long draw. I paid five dollars a bowl. You hold your breath for a while and then you blow out. Then the owner fixes the next bowl, until you tell him that's enough. I'd lie there for hours until I was ready for more. If I wanted to I could order something to drink, or a woman, but mostly people just lay there in a daze. I did it maybe half a dozen times when I was in Vietnam.

When I first arrived in-country, in transit camp, halfway to Phu Loi, I was scared, didn't know anybody, and people were looking at me weird. There was a row of barracks for people just arriving in-country. Across from that was a row of barracks for people going out—people who had already spent a year there. I was walking down this road after chow—all of a sudden I feel something on my leg. It's a fucking monkey on a leash about thirty yards long, leading to a white dude leaning up against the hooch of the guys going out. This motherfucker had a monkey trained to attack Asians! It was very apparent to me right away. So I freaked and tried to grab the monkey, but he jumped off me. Then I started to go for my gun, but they all were packing and I saw what was up, so I just chilled out. That really pissed me off. That kind of thing was not uncommon, though, fortunately for me, most of the time the GIs treated me like another GI, even when they had not been exposed to Asian Americans. There were a few times where they didn't know me or they weren't sure initially that I was a GI, and then they treated me like a gook. I mostly hung with white urban kids, people who were into the counterculture and smoked dope.

I got posters from friends back home, acid, underground papers, and Black Panther newsletters. I think the resentment was ever-present. My anger against the war was mostly repressed yet underlying everything,

and not overtly engaged in. There was a lot of passive-aggressive stuff going on. Part of it was an anti-war sentiment, another part was an anti-Army sentiment—a "Fuck the Army" kind of thing. It's hard to separate the two. It was a stronger sentiment among urban, leftist youth.

Most of the guys in-country were working-class and non-political. Those who were "long-hairs" were more counterculture than anti-war, more reacting to some of the capitalist mentality and value system than to the imperial motivation of the war. For everybody, there was a lot of underlying anger. The popular thing to do was "hide and sham": we wouldn't fix the helicopter the way we were supposed to, or we'd disappear for half a day, or we'd play games like, "Why weren't you here?"—"Well, so-and-so told me I should go over there." We stayed high all the time, got loaded all the time. For one year, every single day we smoked dope all day long, and functioned.

On the other hand, there were the juicers, the drinkers, the country boys, the good 'ole boys, the boys who were into the war, the racists. There was a definite separation between the heads and the juicers. Then there were the blacks. They were caught between reacting to racism and having the power to react, being on an equal power footing with the racists. They were of the attitude, "I'll do my job, but don't fuck with me." There was, in general, a very noticeable hostility among most of the blacks. There were certain exceptions—black officers and black NCOs who were in support capacities. I'm talking about grunts and line units. Everybody was armed and therefore everybody demanded and got respect. Even the racists were careful about expressing anti-black sentiments as well as sentiments toward the leftists or heads.

Women were available everywhere. Phu Loi was a base camp next to a small village. Soc Trang was a helipad and a refueling stop next to a small town. Canto was a city. In Soc Trang we went into the village now and then, but there weren't that many places to go. In Canto there were

streets lined with bars and women. That's where I met this woman, who had a family, lived in town, and rolled grass. We bought grass from her, and after a couple of visits she let us hang out at her house. We would play with her kids and order food, drink, and women, and she would send her daughter out to score. She'd make a little bit off the side. That was the most normal exposure to Vietnamese people I had. All other contacts involved either hooch maids who were selling dope or sex or scamming cigarettes, or whores in bars.

I felt no overt racism toward myself unless I didn't have my uniform on and was caught walking down the road—then I was just another gook. I was treated like an American, except for one or two occasions where a whore kind of sneered at me. I got the feeling she was sneering at me because I was Asian and not white. She wanted money and I wouldn't give it to her.

As far as being Asian, I think the hardest part of the war was not so much any particular incident or experience but the knowledge of a latent racist activity going on all around me on a day-by-day basis. Everytime I saw some drunk GI kick a Vietnamese girl, it reminded me that the GI was kicking her because she was Asian, a gook; if she were white, the GI would not be doing that. If Vietnam were Germany, this overt racism would not have happened.

I saw this type of overt violence all the time. A GI in a bad mood or drunk takes it out on the Vietnamese—gook this, slut that. Then he'd come back and get yelled at by the sergeant and turn around and cuss out the hooch maid: "You didn't shine my shoes right; where's my god-damn towel?" We would be riding down the road on the back of deuce-and-a-half and the drivers would throw shit at people on the road or swerve toward them to scare the shit out of them. I never saw a GI shoot at

anybody from a truck, but I've seen it out of choppers. We would be flying along and a GI would take some shots at somebody below in the field for the hell of it.

I stayed loaded and tried not to notice and tried to not let it get to me. To fight, to protest, to react, was one of those futile urges that, in the end, accomplishes nothing. Would it make me feel better? Not really. I reacted like a Buddha-head; that's how I coped. In our culture we are told that we have to have self-discipline, that we have to suppress our reactions and feelings: *Shikataganai*—"It can't be helped." I'd say that those kind of cultural things equipped me to deal with and cope with shit like that. When that wouldn't work, I used the dope. There was always a degree of racism lying dormant right there on the edge, right on the brink. With racist reactions a breath away, it really felt kind of dangerous. I didn't always know who all of these people were; I didn't always know what had just happened to them this morning or yesterday. So there was always a bit of danger in speaking out. Somebody's friend got killed the day before and here I am; as far as he is concerned I'm another gook. If I say something—well, you never know. Everybody is armed; everybody can kill; everybody's scared and pissed off.

I never carried my M16, but I had a .25 caliber pistol and a switchblade that I kept when I went off base. In Can Tho they took all of our weapons because some blacks tried to kill a sergeant and it was decided that, since the base camp was secure, they'd pull all the weapons. Everyone just went out on the black market and got rearmed. The M16 that we just turned in was available on the black market. It was kind of stupid, because our M16s were confiscated but not the .60 caliber machine guns from the choppers. If shit happened, I would have to use my chopper machine gun rather than my M16. It was pretty fucking dumb.

Racism was something I was constantly aware of and pained about during my time in Vietnam. Whenever I saw GIs mistreating the

MELVIN WADACHI

Vietnamese, I would identify with the Vietnamese and start to work up my anger, only to have to repress it again. I think probably the most painful experience was when I first got there. A new hooch maid had started working with the US Army in Vietnam at about the same time that I arrived. When our unit moved from Phu Loi to Soc Trang, she moved with us because that was the only way she could get by. I think most of the hooch maids probably did also. When I first met her, she was young, fresh-faced, shy and polite, and trying to do everything she could to help the guys. By the time we got to Soc Trang, she was turning tricks. She went from buying American cigarettes and selling them on the black market—buying at our cost then tripling the money on the black market—to selling dope. By the time I left she looked like—the only analogy I can think of is that when we first arrived in-country, we were the fresh green troops; and then there were all these ragged, grizzled, one-year veterans stumbling out the other side—something along that line. She was fresh-faced and innocent when I first arrived, and by the time I left she was haggard and beat-up. It was really sad. Seeing that happening over the course of that year was one of the most painful experiences for me.

I did some flying when I was in Soc Trang. That was the Vietnamization period, so we flew scouts, gunships, and slicks to take men into the battle zone and take out the dead and wounded. I guess I flew for about a month. We flew out to the ARVN base, loaded up the troops, flew out to the combat zone, inserted the troops, came out, and then sat out most of the day. The war starts early in the morning and the troops fight all day; we would sit and fuck around about an hour or two away from the combat. Our scouts would be flying and fighting and our gunships would be supporting. But the slicks, which was what I was flying in, would just sit it out. As the sun went down, we would go back and get the troops. There were a few times when we took fire, and there were a few times

we'd barely had a chance to get the ARVNs out because the VC were so close.

I was at Soc Trang when Nixon ordered the invasion of Cambodia. Our company was sent up to the border. I didn't go across, but our troops did. We flew out to the border and set up a maintenance and refueling post, but by that time it was mostly the Vietnamese who were doing the fighting. So we sat on the border while the ships flew out, did their war thing and came back, and then we'd refuel and rearm them. During that period there was a lot of shit being brought out of Cambodia. Choppers returned with gold, money, art pieces, shit like that, mostly carried by US officers. Also, the Air America choppers were flying back and forth. It wasn't until a week later, when they pulled us back and stuck us in Soc Trang, that the fixed-wing Air America planes came in. It was one of those days I was out on the flight line inspecting a chopper when a fixed-wing came in and unloaded bundles. I asked the guys, "What's going on?" and they said, "Don't you know? That's the opium from the golden triangle." Air America brought opium from across Cambodia. I don't *know* if that's true, but it was fairly widespread, and everyone believed that the CIA was involved with the opium trade.

That's only one small part of the story of ripping off and scamming I saw in Vietnam. I met a twenty-two-year-old American kid who bought a hotel in Vung Tau by selling dope. He was shipping grass back to America in elephant-end table statues, and he made enough money to buy a hotel in Vung Tau. He was discharged in Vietnam and stayed there. I also met this Indonesian sergeant who spoke half a dozen languages, including Vietnamese. He came to America for the sole purpose of joining the Army so he could go to Vietnam as an American GI. As an active Army GI, he had access to all of the Army's economic power. He had a scam where he hired a Vietnamese heating and refrigerator repairman in town

who would sabotage the air conditioner; then he'd tell the officer that he could get it fixed in town. He'd take it to town, get it fixed, get paid, and get his cut. He was rotating air conditioners—there were hundreds of thousands of air conditioners in Vietnam. Imagine rotating two or three a month! He had a good scam going.

He did the same thing with auto parts and vehicle parts. There were all kinds of needs—equipment, supplies, this and that—and with his ability to speak the various languages, he was in an excellent position to place himself as a middle man. He made hundreds of thousands of dollars. He was also sending gold leaf taped to the bodies of women to Switzerland. The deal was that they would take his gold and deposit it in a Swiss bank. In return, they would get a ticket to Paris, which was their way out. That was how he got his money out. This guy was a real operator. I couldn't believe that this guy was a staff sergeant in the US Army. He probably made hundreds of thousands, maybe millions, of dollars on those kinds of scams.

I met another sergeant who ran the motor pool. He sold deuce-and-a-half truck tires worth $1,000 a piece to the Vietnamese. He'd throw all this shit in the truck and just drive out and sell it to the Vietnamese.

I was just a dope fiend—angry, somewhat depressed, and paranoid. I don't remember the pain and fear as much these days, but I think back to the fun shit we did. The last two weeks in Vietnam I shipped all kinds of shit home, like cameras and stereos. I had accumulated four or five different kinds of cameras, huge speakers, and stereos. I opened everything and stuck all kinds of stuff—opium, speed, and grass—into the components before I shipped them home.

I lived in the garage for eight months

I left Vietnam and returned home in December of 1970. I was filled with anxiety, tension, and excitement about coming home. About two weeks

before my date to return, I stopped working. I'd say, "Sorry, Sarg, I've got something to do." I just hung around the beach, got high, caught some sun, and ate. Every now and then, they would send somebody over to make me go inspect this or sign off that. Then it was time to go, and I remember trying to be patient going through the transition camps and standing in lines and getting paperwork done. Finally we flew into Oakland at night. I didn't know anybody but made my way to San Francisco airport. I didn't have my uniform on because, on my last day in-country, I piled my uniform in a heap outside the hooch and set it on fire with lighter fluid.

It was strange landing in Oakland. I didn't even know where I was and I didn't know where I wanted to go. I just focused on going home. I got a five-day early out; after they saw that they couldn't get any work out of me, they recut my orders. I got back five days earlier than my folks had expected. For whatever reason, I never made the effort to tell my folks exactly when I was coming home. Maybe it was because I needed the space to walk into the house when I was really ready, because I was a little unsure how that was going to be. I caught a cab, got to my folks' house—feeling really strange, like I was from another time—and knocked on the door. My mom opened it and started crying, and my dad was teary-eyed, too. It was strange because my folks seemed so different, so alien and far away. They were being themselves, but I'd been exposed to so much shit that I had changed. I felt very different. Even talking to them was real anxiety-producing. It just took some time to readjust to the world.

I moved into the garage, not into my old bedroom. My dad had separated half the garage into an office/storeroom, and I moved in there. The garage was like the hooch in Vietnam, because it was a little raw; it wasn't carpeted and had rough wood walls. I had taken a single fold-out bed that was almost like a cot, which I slept on for about a year. I had no running water, but I had a plastic bottle for holding water, like I did in

Nam. I felt comfortable in the garage. I would eat with my folks and spend time with them—but not too much, a couple of hours—and then I'd go back there to the garage. I lived in the garage for eight months. My folks were concerned but tolerant.

I think the fear, anger, and blatant racism—those kinds of raw feelings and experiences that I had never experienced before the war—made me paranoid and angry. When I got back to civilization, where being on the edge and being defensive and having to be ready to do something are no longer necessary, it took some time to calm down, to be human again. The hardest part was reconciling the racism. Before Nam I had hung out with a lot of whites and Mexicans, but after Nam I just didn't feel right around them. When I went back to school in 1972, I was lucky to find that the Asian American movement had reached Cal State Northridge and there was an Asian American student group office on campus. I met a Japanese American woman I fell in love with, and we started dating. It took me a while to relearn how to act toward women, but she helped me become human again.

I haven't associated with whites, except tangentially, since returning from Nam. I used to date white girls before Nam, but since returning I've dated only Asian women. I'm married to a Japanese woman now. I can't say I hate whites but, even after making the adjustment back to the world, I feel no need or desire to reintegrate myself with them. It's not so much an unwillingness or a not wanting to; when I work with whites now, I think it's an even relationship. Not only did I need to deal with the racist experiences, which apparently could only be done in an ethnic context, but also having chosen the line of work that I do keeps me in the ethnic community.

After I finished my undergraduate degree, I was recruited into UCLA's masters program in social work. The recruiting aspect was part of affirmative action, which was alive and well. I was an older Asian who'd had life experience, and being mature made me sought after by student

groups that were trying to recruit activist people. There was the expectation that I would play an advocacy role for Asian civic issues. That expectation set me on a particular track. Getting a job as a counselor blended all of those experiences, perspectives, and philosophies. I sometimes wonder if I'm still here because I hate whites, because I haven't reconciled my shit about the war. But I really don't think so. I feel that I am a positive and constructive person, and that my work is an affirmation of who I am and what I am and what I want to do. I'm an activist who is trying to change the system to maximize benefits for the community. Those ideas guide most of my community activities today.

CHAPTER ELEVEN

CURTIS KITAGAWA

ARMY, 1970-71

CAMP EVANS

I was slowly becoming a hippie

My dad was born in Riverside, California and grew up in Pasadena, California, graduating from John Muir High School and Pasadena City College. He became a gardener just like his grandfather, who was a gardener and landscaper in Pasadena. My dad's family were imprisoned in Gila River, Arizona during World War II. He met my mother in Chicago, where his family went in search of work when they were released from camp. I was born in 1948 in Chicago. We moved to Pasadena when I was three years old, and a few years after that we moved to East Los Angeles. In the summer of 1959, when I was in the fifth grade, we moved to Whittier, California. My father's gardening business became successful in Whittier and he expanded his business to include selling and servicing gardening equipment.

I first encountered racism as a kid living in Whittier. There was one other Japanese kid going to my elementary school with my brother and myself. Given our age group, most of our parents had been through World War II, and many of the dads had fought in the Pacific and lost

family members in the war fighting the Japanese, so there wasn't a lot of compassion for the Japanese Americans living in Whittier. In this atmosphere, it wasn't uncommon to be called a Jap or to be referred to as the Yellow Peril by other kids. One interesting experience that occurred in Whittier was that the father of one of my friends, who had fought in the Pacific Islands as a Marine Corps infantryman, ended up in Japan during the occupation. He and his family understood and loved Japanese culture; they knew more about Japanese culture than *my* family. But this was really the exception in Whittier.

I first heard about Laos and Vietnam in the early 1960s when I was taking a social studies class in junior high school. I remember watching a newsreel about Southeast Asia in class. At that time the war wasn't in Vietnam but in Laos, and I distinctly remember the social science teacher saying, "What do we call the people in Laos? Louses? That doesn't sound right." I remember that incident because around that period I was beginning to become aware of kids in school making fun of other people because of their ethnicity. Whittier was a strongly right-wing, church-oriented, white community of predominantly working- and middle-class people.

In this classroom newsreel I recall seeing American military advisors in Laos and the Laotian military wearing American uniforms; it was what we would call today "covert action." The newsreel showed interviews with Laotians and Americans saying that Laos was the new hotspot in the world. That was my first knowledge of Southeast Asia and it really stuck in my mind. Our teacher spent one or two classes talking about where Laos was located and said that the area was once called Indochina and that the French had once occupied the nation. In high school I was oblivious to current events; I didn't read the newspaper, nor did I watch the war being fought on the evening news.

I knew I had to register at age eighteen for the draft, so that made me cognizant that there was a war going on. I also knew that staying in school was the best way to get a deferment from the draft. Out of high school my aspiration was to attend the University of Southern California to study ceramics, but I didn't have the grades to go there. I ended up going to a community college and in my second year, near the end of 1968, I got my draft notice. I got a temporary delay because my dad had neck surgery and had to be flat on his back for a month. I always worked for my dad at his shop on weekends and summers, so I got a deferment for hardship to work in the family business. When I went up for the hardship case, I asked for my 2-S deferment. They gave me one for another six months, which would expire if I didn't go on to a four-year college. I lost my deferment in the summer of 1969.

By the summer of 1969, "flower power" was coming on strong and I was slowly becoming a hippie as my hair grew longer. I definitely felt a part of the counterculture. I was into the art crowd by 1969, doing ceramics, singing folk music, and drinking a lot of Red Mountain and Japanese plum wines. I was taught in school that dope was bad and not to mess with it, but most of my friends were just starting to smoke pot and so I started smoking pot just before I went to Vietnam. I was a late bloomer!

I took a trip to Michigan to visit my relatives before going to basic training. My uncle said he had friends who could get me to Nova Scotia to beat the draft. He wasn't outwardly against the war, but he had sympathies with the anti-war group. He didn't want his nephew to get blown away for nothing. He felt that Vietnam was not worth fighting for. I must have been feeling quasi-macho and stupid, because I told my uncle that I wanted to go to Vietnam. The draft notice showed up while I was in Michigan and I had to report by September 1969. I wasn't watching the news, and so I was still oblivious to what was happening in Vietnam.

My family didn't discuss the fact that there was a war going on and

that I would be a participant. It was more that the Army might straighten me out and make a man out of me. By that summer of 1969 I had become a highly visible member of the counterculture: I wore mariachi sandals and jeans, my hair had grown long, I had love beads strung around my neck, and I had started smoking grass. The Vietnam War was still a distant affair that was going on somewhere in Asia. I wasn't a draft protester then, in the summer of 1969: I was just a hippie; I was into love, peace, having fun, and enjoying the music. I played my guitar and started getting more into painting and sculpting. My dad, who is a very strict person and a Republican, told me that the Army might be good for me. He didn't appreciate my hippie lifestyle.

My father was concerned that he might not see me again

I went to Fort Ord, California for nine weeks of basic training in September of 1969. There was one other Asian from Malaysia. I didn't get harassed for being Asian American. The platoon leader of our training company was a former busted gang leader and he was made the platoon leader because the DIs thought he had leadership abilities. There were some really smart and some really dumb people in our platoon. It didn't matter who you were or who you thought you were, in basic training you were a maggot trainee.

The head mess sergeant in basic training in charge of the mess hall was a Japanese American guy. At graduation, my family and friends showed up and my father approached the head mess sergeant and asked him if he could get me a place in the mess hall working for him. It had finally dawned on my father that I was probably going to Vietnam. The idea my dad had that the Army might make a man out of me turned into the possibility of my getting killed and him losing his only son. In the end, the cook couldn't do anything.

After basic training I went to Fort Hood, Texas and got attached to the

2nd Armored Division, Headquarters Company, 6th Squadron of the 1st Cavalry Regiment. The cavalry unit consisted of tanks, APCs, helicopters, and a company of grunts. They didn't have a place for me for a month, so I was made barracks guard during that time. I got assigned as RTO (radio telephone operator) to a captain who was studying penetration exercises there. I did that in the field for a month. After two months at Fort Hood, I made Spec 4 and got orders for Vietnam in September of 1970.

My family had asked me what I wanted to do for my last week of vacation before I left for Vietnam. We all flew up to Seattle, spent money, took the ferry to the islands, and had a nice time together. My parents weren't intimate with their kids other than lecturing them about things; we weren't the huggy-kissy types, but we all hugged before I left. I sensed that my father was concerned that he might not see me again.

I became known as the Green Hornet

I arrived in Vietnam in September of 1970. I had just broken up with my girlfriend in Berkeley because she said she wouldn't wait for me. The plane, World Airways, landed in Cam Ranh Bay at dusk. We flew to Danang from Cam Ranh Bay and then trucked to Camp Evans. We traveled on semi-trucks, with two people up front armed with M16s. I was nervous sitting in the rear of the truck because I didn't have a weapon. Highway One was a secure road during the day, but at night the VC owned it. It was a couple of hours' drive and I saw mostly open fields, not rice paddies or villages. The rules of the road were that the bigger you were, the more rights you had to drive on it. No one wanted to stop on the road because then you were a target for frags. Once I arrived at "Screaming Eagle" replacement center, I went through in-country jungle training for about a week. There were a few comments made to me during jungle training to the effect of "You look just like a

gook" from the trainers who had been there for a while, but I didn't say anything. I eventually ended up with the 101st Airborne Division at Camp Evans. The guys had just come in from the field and were on stand-down. I was one of about thirty replacements for a line company.

I volunteered for point on our first patrol outside the base perimeter, but I ended up walking point with another guy. We had a cherry lieutenant in our platoon plus three veterans of combat in Vietnam, and the rest were new in-country. I was the only Asian in my platoon and I was told that if I came across a VC walking point, the VC would probably stop and look at me because I was Asian and that that should give me a half-second to drop him. I was told this after I had been walking point for about a week. I promptly traded walking point with another guy walking slack.

One time we got into a viney, dense jungle area and I was taken off point because I was too slow and making too much noise hacking away at the dense jungle growth. I couldn't carry the heavy pack and sling the machete and chop the jungle stuff down to clear a path for the platoon. Getting taken off point was fine with me. Then I was made slack, second to the point man, or rear guard, at the end of the line. The platoon commander felt I had the "eyes" to do this. I became known as the "Green Hornet."

We started having attrition due to dysentery and an occasional booby trap—toe poppers, as they were called—when tripped, a small charge of C4 blew a foot or leg off up to the knee. The traps were in the ground, usually on the other side of a log, where we'd step over the log and put our foot down. They were also on old trails, so we had to cut new trails parallel to the old trails. I remember instances where somebody wanted to go to the back of the line to talk to the lieutenant and stepped onto the old trail and, BOOM, lost a leg. The VC or NVA [North Vietnamese Army] weren't around at this time. This was the beginning of the

Vietnamization of the war by Nixon. What we had were VC trail-watchers—a couple of VC following an hour behind us, which might be only two hundred yards. I remember being watched for a week and finally the VC made contact on day twenty-nine of the patrol. This patrol went on for a straight thirty-one days. We had to carry everything on our backs; for me, it was a lot. I got tired of carrying sandbag fillers; it would rain and the sandbag material kept getting heavier. I also carried my M16 with twenty-one magazines, three frags, one or two smokes, a claymore, a trip flare, a machete, a shovel, a poncho, a poncho liner, a case of C-rations, two quart-sized canteens, an empty M16 ammo can for papers, cigarettes, and a magazine clip in my helmet band. This was in October, when it's hot and dry, just before the monsoons.

I remember the second day on the patrol sleeping on a hillside with a small tree between my legs so I wouldn't slide down the hill, soaking wet, with a poncho over me. Everybody got along just fine as far as the race issue. Everybody worked together because it was all about survival. It was toward the end of the war and it was predominantly draftees. Regardless if you'd gone to NCO school or not, self-preservation—"hide and slide"—was the idea, not "seek and destroy." If we thought there was going to be contact, we would go up a different hill. We would only look for VC if we were ordered to do so.

We had a captain who was on his third tour; he was an E6 on his first tour, went to OCS [Officer Candidate School], came back as a lieutenant, and became captain of our company. He wanted everybody to survive. There weren't any VC or North Vietnamese regulars to make contact with. I don't think the NVA were interested in making contact either. They were probably more interested in getting down the Ho Chi Minh Trail into Saigon. We were up north by the Sang Bo River, about ten

miles east of the Ashau Valley. The previous August our company had been decimated by the NVA on fire base O'Reilley, which had 105-howitzers firing into the valley. We were the replacements for the remnants of that battalion.

We had contact on that first patrol. We saw the VC when we were picked up by helicopter and moved to another location; we weren't allowed to fire from the helicopter. I think those were the VC that were our trail-watchers.

I remember being out in the field, dug in on a defensive position, and radioing in for water. Everybody was down to their last canteen and it was 95 degrees. They said that the airfield was socked in with fog—and here we were, sitting in the bright sunshine, baking. I saw helicopters a half mile away dropping leaflets that read, "Turn to the government side, and we'll pay you to be a scout. There's no sense fighting anymore." The helicopter must have taken fire because they began throwing frags out the window. Our lieutenant was yelling on the radio to get the helicopters to drop us some water. Instead of water, we got in-flight rations for the Air Force: a snack—canned fruit with crackers or cakes and a ham sandwich in a can. We were getting upset. You don't eat fruit when you have dysentery; everybody had dysentery because we tried to drink the water out of the streams.

By the end of our thirty-one day patrol our company was down to about a couple dozen healthy guys. All the officers were down with dysentery; our platoon leader, the lieutenant, got sent back to the rear, so there were no officers in the field. A colonel flew out to take charge of the remnants of the platoon, down to thirty people from close to ninety. The colonel put us on stand-down and the VC trail-watchers saw their opportunity. While we were cutting an LZ [landing zone] on a hillside for a helicopter to take us all back to base, we got hit. Our guard was down, the morale was down, and we had been soaking wet for a week with no change of clothes and poor rations. I remember putting C4

around the trees, but the trunks were so hard that the explosion would blow holes in them but wouldn't knock them down. We ended up chopping the trees down with axes and that's when we got hit.

My squad got elected to chase the VC. We never caught the snipers and finally got extracted and returned to the base camp and did a stand-down for two weeks. I had the flu, dysentery, ringworm up both my legs up to my crotch, and jungle rot on my feet. I was a wreck, as was everybody else. The company went back to the field as a platoon after a week. The guys who were sick, including me, stayed behind. I ended up getting a job as a company clerk at Camp Evans.

Camp Evans was huge, bigger than Camp Eagle at Danang, and big enough to land C130s, bigger than Khe Sanh. There were three line battalions with helicopters and fixed-wing spotter planes. As I recall, there was a village north of Camp Evans near the Sang Bo River; we were located south of the river. We got our water from the river, filled it up with chlorine, and used it for washing, maybe brushing teeth, but *not* to drink—the water was brown like urine. We all drank sodas or beer.

Local Vietnamese civilians ran two laundries on base. It was rumored that one of the guys working in the laundry was VC, because we never got our own clothes back. We always ended up with someone else's clothes—especially me, since I was so small and my clothes would fit other small people.

We lived in hooches made of plywood with screens on the sides and positioned up on stilts surrounded by sandbags. A hooch would sleep two rows of canvas cots, about thirty people. We used a poncho liner and poncho for bed cover. If it was cold and rainy, we had plastic sheeting to cover the screens. We didn't have hooch maids because they had caught an old *papa-san* pacing off from headquarters to whatever; they could walk mortars into the bunkers or the radios. All the local Vietnamese

civilians were thrown off the base and only those hired to work were allowed into the base. Toward the end of my tour, it got to be so civilized that we had a steam-and-cream massage parlor on base. For 35 cents we could take a shower and then go into a private cubby hole, a row of closets, where a Vietnamese girl would give a massage. If you had extra money you could probably get some sex, but I never did because the dividers between the cells were so low, you could stand up and look over.

There was a lot of marijuana, opium, and heroin at Camp Evans in 1970 when I was there. The marijuana came pre-rolled in cigarette papers, with ten cigarettes per package in a plastic waterproof wrapper, called a "deck," for only one dollar. Later on I saw some that had a faint blue pinstriping down one side; that grass would make you grit your teeth when smoked—the guys said that it was laced with speed.

We could also get raw brown liquid opium, sold in small vials about the size of my little finger, three-quarters of an inch long, one-half inch in diameter with a small, black plastic cap. We brushed the opium on our joints or on our cigarettes and smoked it. The black guys called heroin "their" drug, while marijuana was considered the white man's drug. As I recall, not many blacks smoked grass; they mostly shot heroin. Vietnamese heroin was very pure. A small vial of heroin sold for five dollars in Vietnam; back in the States the same vial would have cost one hundred dollars or more for only 25 percent pure; in Vietnam the heroin wasn't cut, it was *very* pure.

The Vietnamese who worked at the base would bring the drugs in through the gate when they came in to work—cleaning the hooches, cleaning the mess halls, doing laundry—in the mornings. During the day, while we repaired the perimeter wire or just hung around, they'd come up to us and sell us the dope.

Some of the guys would have LSD sent to them from friends back home. My first trip was in Vietnam. I took something called "Orange Sunshine"—a paper blotter acid as big and thick as a thumbnail. I

remember I had a headache and a bummer of a trip, but my friend was running up and down the compound screaming, "Wow, this is great!"

When the guys came back out of the field, we'd all get together and party, with bowls and joints passing around the hooch—fifteen to eighteen guys smoking grass, or whatever, in the hooch at one time. Once, the captain came in with a lieutenant to announce a stand-down and a steak dinner for chow. Everybody dropped the pipes, bowls, and joints they were holding. Our hooch was covered in a thick cloud of smoke. The officers didn't say a word. From that time on I was watched, because they thought I was the dope supplier, since I worked in the office, which was in the rear, and I was always at the dope parties. I didn't have to be a supplier because it was available everywhere on base. We could have any kind of drug we wanted; the only thing missing [then] was women. Women were not allowed in our compound area. I think that drug use was tolerated because we couldn't have any women on base.

By 1970 black guys would flash the clenched fist like the Black Panthers— fist up—and do the "dap," knocking fists; we all did it. Guys were wearing peace signs on their helmets and carving FTA, "Fuck the Army," on hooch walls. By then I'd been in Vietnam for six months, and we all had to turn in our weapons to the armory after a couple of companies got drunk and started shooting at each other in the barracks after returning from the field.

We talked about the war, sitting in our hooches and getting high, but we never talked about what the purpose of the war was. We discussed the war as soldiers in war. I remember when Khe Sanh was about to be reopened to block the NVA from coming south, we got this gung-ho captain who needed field time to become a major and therefore wanted to send us on a seek-and-destroy mission. We just wanted to get out and return home, but *he* wanted to take a particular hill. One night his unit

got hit and he called for artillery—six guys from our company got hit from friendly fire. Our morale was completely down, as far as fighting a war was concerned. By 1970 the point was to get home without getting shot.

I got along with both blacks and whites in the rear. The hard-core militant blacks—from Oakland, Harlem, Detroit—considered me to be white. They said they were in Vietnam fighting a white man's war and that they were being made to fight their "yellow brothers." They would claim conscientious objector status and end up at Long Bien jail. One Mexican guy I knew was a CO on religious grounds and refused to carry a weapon.

Sitting stoned inside our hooches, we used to pour alcohol inside a water bottle and drop a match inside. I remember the alcohol fumes would burn in an undulating blue flame—real interesting when you're stoned. We would also get a plastic sheet and tie it into knots, like a rope, and hang it from the hooch ceiling. We'd set the bottom on fire and watch it drip onto the floor. It looked like a mini-gun firing and made a funny "swish" noise as the plastic dripped. We would sit around looking at this as we got high.

In the NCO club on base the country-western guys would be singing shit-kicking music. We had the country-western "get-in-a-fight" guys and the "peaceniks-smoking-dope" guys. The hard-core black guys would disappear into the bunkers, or wherever, to shoot heroin. There were alcoholic guys who would be wasted the whole seven days they were on stand-down. They were the ones who had fights; dopers never got into arguments or caused problems. I didn't have problems with either side. I could go into the NCO club and have a beer. I remember a good 'ole boy from the South talking to me once and telling me that he'd been taught that blacks smelled and looked different because they were inferior and weren't really human beings. This guy had been in the Army for almost two years and had been eating, sleeping, shitting, fighting side by

side, and had come to realize that blacks weren't any different from whites.

I had a good rapport among some of these people. Being Asian, I could float around and fit in and we would talk about anything. I was one of the few who could do that, being a sociable person. Once, a real hard-core cowboy-type guy from Montana called me a gook when I was sitting in the NCO club drinking a beer. I called him an "overgrown albino gorilla from Montana," and he burst out laughing and we became best of friends.

Author's note: Curtis returned to southern California and currently operates a gardening repair and sale store.

AFTERWORD

THE MYTH OF MODEL
MINORITY

During the two decades spanning the end of World War II and the beginning of the Vietnam War, America was a society celebrating domestic affluence and international hegemony.[1] For many Americans, however, the Vietnam War jolted the sense of security and innocence often associated with this mythical image of their country. For Japanese American soldiers in particular, whose sense of American security was already sheared by the experience of their parents' imprisonment during World War II, together with their growing sense of alienation from postwar American society, the war represents the antithesis of the heroic quest, "the triumph over weakness, the promise of salvation, prosperity, and progress."[2]

Many of the veterans in this book might, of course, be considered to represent the classical American success story. Formerly urban youths (some of them gang members) growing up in the midst of postwar economic dislocation, they served in Vietnam for their country and have since come to achieve a certain level of American middle-class affluence. Today many of them, indeed, live in suburban middle-class neighborhoods and are successful professionals in varied careers as accountants, engineers, architects, financial and real estate brokers, bankers, lawyers, small-business owners, and administrators and managers in local city police and fire departments.

But these success stories do not always reflect the persistent and simplistic myth of the model minority often tagged onto the Asian American community. In many cases, the experiences related by the veterans here are responses to an attempt to come to terms with something far more complex—the legacy of a war which continues to reverberate through many of the social and cultural upheavals of the past half-century.

NOTES

INTRODUCTION

1. W. D. Ehrhart, "Last Flight Out from the War Zone" quoted in Vince Gotera, *Radical Visions: Poetry by Vietnam Veterans*. Athens, GE: University of Georgia Press, 1994, p. 275.
2. Thomas J. McCormick, *America's Half-Century: United States Foreign Policy in the Cold War*. Baltimore, MD: John Hopkins Press, 1989, pp. 112–13; William Blum, *Killing Hope: U.S. Military and CIA Interventions since World War II*. Monroe, Maine: Common Courage Press, 1995, p. 122; Gary R. Hess, *Vietnam and the United States: Origins and Legacy of War*. Boston, MA: Twayne, 1990, p. 73; Patrick J. Hearden, *The Tragedy of Vietnam*. New York: HarperCollins, 1991, pp. 99–126.
3. Paul R. Spickard, *Japanese Americans: The Formation and Transformations of an Ethnic Group*. New York: Twayne, 1996, p. 133.
4. Ibid., p. 162.
5. Lisa Lowe, *Immigrant Acts: On Asian American Cultural Politics*. Durham, NC: Duke University Press, 1996, p. 6; Spickard, *Japanese Americans*, p. 2.
6. Spickard, *Japanese Americans*, p. 93.
7. Quoted in ibid., p. 94.
8. Ronald T. Tsukashima, "Continuity of Ethnic Participation in the Economy: Immigrants in Contract Gardening." *Amerasia Journal* 21:3 (Winter 1995/1996), p. 53.
9. Spickard, *Japanese Americans*, p. 135.

10. Tsukashima, "Continuity of Ethnic Participation", p. 54.
11. Mike Davis, *City of Quartz*. London: Verso, 1990, p. 43.
12. Spickard, *Japanese Americans*, p. 90; David J. O'Brien and Stephen S. Fujita, *The Japanese American Experience*. Indianapolis, IN: Indiana University Press, 1991, p. 63.
13. William Wei, *The Asian American Movement*. Philadelphia, PA: Temple University Press, 1993, p. 14.
14. William E. Merritt, *Where the River Ran Backward*. New York: Anchor Books, 1989, p. 17.
15. Ron Kovic, *Born on the Fourth of July*. New York: Pocket Books, 1976, p. 76.
16. Christian G. Appy, *Working-Class War: American Combat Soldiers and Vietnam*. Chapel Hill, NC: University of North Carolina, 1993, p. 87.
17. Ibid., p. 117.
18. Frederick Downs, *The Killing Zone: My Life in the Vietnam War*. New York: Berkeley Books, 1978, p. 31.
19. Richard Moser, *The New Winter Soldiers: GI and Veteran Dissent during the Vietnam Era*. New Brunswick, NJ: Rutgers University Press, 1996, p. 63.
20. Ibid., p. 41.
21. Philip Caputo, *Rumors of War*. New York: Holt, Rineheart and Winston, 1977, p. xiv.
22. Ibid., p. xiv.
23. Charley Trujillo, *Soldados: Chicanos in Viet Nam*. San Jose, CA: Chusma House Publications, 1990, p. 179.
24. Wei, *The Asian American Movement*, p. 41.
25. Appy, *Working-Class War*, p. 299.

AFTERWORD

1. McCormick, *America's Half-Century*, p. 1.
2. Lowe, *Immigrant Acts*, pp. 2–3.

SELECT BIBLIOGRAPHY

ASIAN AMERICAN STUDIES

Bernstein, Joan Z. *Personal Justice Denied: Report of the Commission on Wartime Relocation and Internment of Civilians.* Seattle, WA: University of Washington Press, 1997.

Hata, Donald T. and Nadine I. Hata. *Japanese Americans and World War II: Exclusion, Internment, and Redress.* Wheeling, IL: Harlan Davidson, 1995.

Hong, Maria. *Growing up Asian American.* New York: Avon Books, 1993.

Lowe, Lisa. *Immigrant Acts: On Asian American Cultural Politics.* Durham, NC: Duke University Press, 1996.

O'Brien, David J. and Stephen S. Fujita. *The Japanese American Experience.* Indianapolis, IN: Indiana University Press, 1991.

Okihiro, Gary Y. *Margins and Mainstreams: Asians in American History and Culture.* Seattle, WA: University of Washington Press, 1994.

Spickard, Paul R. *Japanese Americans: The Formation and Transformations of an Ethnic Group.* New York: Twayne, 1996.

Takaki, Ronald. *Strangers from a Different Shore: A History of Asian Americans.* New York: Penguin Books, 1989.

Tsukashima, Ronald T. "Continuity Ethnic Participation in the Economy: Immigrants in Contract Gardening." *Amerasia Journal* 21:3 (winter 1995/1996), pp. 53–76.

Wei, William. *The Asian American Movement.* Philadelphia, PA: Temple University Press, 1993.

VIETNAM WAR NOVELS

Caputo, Philip. *Rumours of War*. New York: Holt, Rinehart and Winston, 1977.

Downs, Frederick. *The Killing Zone: My Life in the Vietnam War*. New York: Berkeley Books, 1978.

Dye, Dale A. *Platoon*. New York: Charter Books, 1986.

Hasford, Gustav. *The Short Timers*. New York: Bantam Books, 1979.

Heinemann, Larry. *Paco's Story*. New York: Penguin Books, 1987.

Herr, Michael. *Dispatches*. New York: Vintage Books, 1991.

Kovic, Ron. *Born on the Fourth of July*. New York: Pocket Books, 1976.

VIETNAM WAR ORAL HISTORIES

Addison Gallery of American Art. *A Matter of Conscience: GI Resistance during the Vietnam War*. Andover, MA: Phillips Academy, 1992.

Baker, Mark. *Nam*. New York: William Morrow and Company, 1981.

Freeman, James M. *Hearts of Sorrow: Vietnamese-American Lives*. Stanford, CA: Stanford University Press, 1989.

Goff, Stanley, and Robert Sanders. *Brothers: Black Soldiers in the Nam*. Novato, CA: Presidio Press, 1982.

Hess, Martha. *Then the Americans Came: Voices from Vietnam*. New Brunswick, NJ: Rutgers University Press, 1994.

Lehrack, Otto J. *No Shining Armor: The Marines at War in Vietnam*. Lawrence, KA: University Press of Kansas, 1992.

Marshall, Kathryn. *In the Combat Zone: An Oral History of American Women in Vietnam*. Boston, MA: Little, Brown and Company, 1987.

Santoli, Al. *Everything We Had*. New York: Ballantine Books, 1981.

Terry, Wallace. *Bloods: An Oral History of the Vietnam War by Black Veterans*. New York: Ballantine Books, 1984.

Tollefson, James W. *The Strength Not to Fight: An Oral History of*

Conscientious Objectors of the Vietnam War. Boston, MA: Little, Brown and Company, 1993.

Trujillo, Charley. *Soldados: Chicanos in Viet Nam.* San Jose, CA: Chusma House Publications, 1990.

VIETNAM WAR STUDIES

Anderegg, Michael. *Inventing Vietnam: The War in Film and Television.* Philadelphia, PA: Temple University Press, 1991.

Appy, Christian G. *Working-Class War: American Combat Soldiers and Vietnam.* Chapel Hill, NC: University of North Carolina, 1993.

Gotera, Vince. *Radical Visions: Poetry by Vietnam Veterans.* Athens, GE: University of Georgia Press, 1994.

Hearden, Patrick J. *The Tragedy of Vietnam.* New York: HarperCollins, 1991.

Hellmann, John. *American Myth and the Legacy of Vietnam.* New York: Columbia University Press, 1986.

Hess, Gary R. *Vietnam and the United States: Origins and Legacy of War.* Boston, MA: Twayne, 1990.

Jason, Philip K. *Fourteen Landing Zones: Approaches to Vietnam War Literature.* Iowa City, IO: University of Iowa Press, 1991.

Knoll, Erwin and Judith N. McFadden. *War Crimes and the American Conscience.* New York: Holt, Rinehart and Winston, 1970.

Kolko, Gabriel. *Anatomy of War: Vietnam, the United States, and the Modern Historical Experience.* New York: Pantheon Books, 1985.

Lang, Daniel. *Casualties of War.* New York: McGraw-Hill, 1969.

MacPherson, Myra. *Long Time Passing: Vietnam and the Haunted Generation.* New York: Anchor Books, 1984.

Marr, David G. *Vietnam 1945: The Quest for Power.* Berkeley, CA: University of California Press, 1995.

Merritt, William E. *Where the Rivers Ran Backward.* New York: Anchor Books, 1989.

Moser, Richard. *The New Winter Soldiers: GI and Veteran Dissent during the Vietnam Era.* New Brunswick, NJ: Rutgers University Press, 1996.

Moss, George D. *Vietnam: An American Ordeal.* Englewood Cliffs, NJ: Prentice Hall, 1994.

Rowe, John C., and Rick Berg. *The Vietnam War and American Culture.* New York: Columbia University Press, 1991.

Schulzinger, Robert D. *A Time for War: The United States and Vietnam, 1941–1975.* New York: Oxford University Press, 1997.

Shay, Jonathan. *Achilles in Vietnam: Combat Trauma and the Undoing of Character.* New York: Simon and Schuster, 1994.

Turner, Fred. *Echoes of Combat: The Vietnam War in American Memory.* New York: Anchor Books, 1996.

Vietnam Veterans Against the War. *The Winter Soldier Investigation: An Inquiry into American War Crimes.* Boston, MA: Beacon Press, 1972.

RELATED INTEREST

Blum, William. *Killing Hope: U.S. Military and CIA Interventions since World War II.* Monroe, Maine: Common Courage Press, 1995.

Chomsky, Noam. *Year 501: The Conquest Continues.* Boston, MA: South End Press, 1993.

Davis, Mike. *City of Quartz.* London: Verso, 1990.

Foucault, Michel. *Discipline and Punishment: The Birth of the Prison.* New York: Vintage Books, 1979.

Kimmel, Michael. *Manhood in America: A Cultural History.* New York: Free Press, 1996.

Klein, Malcolm W. *The American Street Gang.* New York: Oxford University Press, 1995.

McCormick, Thomas J. *America's Half-Century: United States Foreign Policy in the Cold War*. Baltimore, MD: Johns Hopkins Press, 1989.

Miller, Timothy. *The Hippies and American Values*. Knoxville, TN: University of Tennessee Press, 1991.

Morgan, Edward. *The Sixties Experience: Hard Lessons about Modern America*. Philadelphia, PA: Temple University Press, 1991.

Palladino, Grace. *Teenagers: An American History*. New York: Basic Books, 1996.

Roszak, Theodore. *The Making of a Counter Culture*. New York: Anchor Books, 1969.

CHRONOLOGY

208 BC   Chinese Han Dynasty expands into Vietnam.

AD 938   Vietnam gains independence from Chinese domination.

1802   Nguyen dynasty unifies Vietnam and establishes capital in Hue.

1846   French Catholic missionaries arrive in Vietnam.

1847   French bombardment of Danang.

1858   French capture Danang.

1859   French capture and occupy Saigon.

1867   French establish direct rule over Cochinchina.

1869   One of the first groups of Japanese contract laborers brought to Hawaii as sugar plantation workers.

1884   Large-scale contract immigration of Japanese workers to Hawaii begins.

1890   Nguyen Sinh Cung (Ho Chi Minh) born.
         First recorded acts of violence against Japanese in San Francisco.
         1890 census records 1,147 Japanese residing in California.

1896   Los Angeles has approximately 100 Japanese residents and 16 Japanese-owned restaurants.

1903   Japanese and Mexican sugar-beet workers strike in Oxnard, California.

1905   Japanese victory over the Russians in the Sino-Japanese War.

1912   Nguyen Sinh Cung leaves Vietnam for the next 30 years.

1913   Alien Land Act passed in California, restricting ownership of land by Japanese.

1914   World War I.

1919   While living in France, Nguyen Sinh Cung changes his name to Nguyen Ai Quoc (Nguyen the Patriot). Attempts to petition delegates at the Versailles conference to grant Vietnam self-determination end in failure.

1920   Ho Chi Minh joins in the founding of the French Communist Party.

1924   California Immigration Act of 1924 ends immigration of all Asian groups to the United States.

1930   Ho Chi Minh, together with Le Duc Tho and Pham Van Dong, creates the Communist Party of Indochina.

       Global economic depression.

       Japanese American Citizens League (JACL) founded.

1932   Bao Dai placed in power by the French to rule over Vietnam.

1939   World War II.

1940   France occupied by Germany. Japanese Army assumes military control of French Indochina.

       Los Angeles County has largest population of Japanese Americans in the US, followed by Seattle, Washington.

1941   Ho Chi Minh creates the Vietminh as an umbrella resistance organization against the French and Japanese in Indochina.

       United States declares war on Japan.

       FBI arrests 1,300 *issei* Japanese Americans on the night of December 7, 1941 (Pearl Harbor attack).

1942   Executive Order 9066 issued, placing 110,000 Japanese (70,000 American-born citizens) and Japanese Americans along the West Coast into military internment camps for the duration of the war.

1943   US Army begins "voluntary" draft of Japanese American men held in internment camps, forming segregated Army units for combat.

1945   Vietminh takes control of Indochina.

       Ho Chi Minh proclaims Vietnamese independence and estab-

lishes Democratic Republic of Vietnam. US President Truman supports French interest in reimposing colonialism in Vietnam.

1946   France reclaims Vietnam as a colony. Vietminh and French forces begin French-Vietminh War.

1947   India and Pakistan gain independence from Britain.

1950   China and the Soviet Union recognize the Democratic Republic of Vietnam under Ho Chi Minh.

US gives recognition to Bao Dai's French-dominated state.

1951   US gives direct economic aid to Bao Dai and military aid to French in Indochina.

1954   French forces defeated at Dien Bien Phu, bringing an end to French colonial rule in Vietnam. The Geneva Conference on Indochina temporarily divides Vietnam at the 17th parallel, pending elections for reunification.

1955   Ngo Dinh Diem ousts Bao Dai and becomes president of the "Republic of Vietnam," otherwise known as South Vietnam. Diem rejects the Geneva agreements for popular elections to be held in 1956 throughout Vietnam.

US begins military assistance directly to Diem.

1960   John F. Kennedy becomes president of the US.

US has approximately 900 military advisors in Vietnam. National Liberation Front (NLF) created.

1961   US military advisors in Vietnam total 3,200.

1962   US military advisors in Vietnam now 12,000.

Strategic-hamlet program initiated.

1963   Buddhist riots begin in Hue, resulting in martial law and arrest of 1,400 Buddhists.

CIA supports assassination of Diem. US military advisors in Vietnam total 16,300.

President Kennedy assassinated.

1964   Passage of the Gulf of Tonkin Resolution by US Congress,

authorizing President Johnson to commit the US to war in Vietnam.

US troop strength in Vietnam reaches 23,300.

1965   US begins bombing of Vietnam in operation code-named "Rolling Thunder."

Two US Marine Corps battalions arrive in Vietnam to reinforce Danang airbase.

First "teach-in" held at the University of Michigan at Ann Arbor.

US troop strength in Vietnam reaches 184,300.

1966   Buddhists and students protest in Hue.

US troop strength in Vietnam reaches 385,300.

1967   US troop strength in Vietnam reaches 485,300.

1968   Asian American Political Alliance (AAPA) started at San Francisco State College.

Tet Offensive.

US Army unit kills 347 men, women, and children in Vietnamese hamlet of My Lai.

Paris Peace Conference begins.

Nixon elected president of the US.

US troop strength reaches 535,000.

1969   US begins secret bombing of Cambodia.

Ho Chi Minh dies at age 79.

Gidra, a radical Asian American alternative newspaper, founded in Los Angeles.

250,000 demonstrate against the war in Vietnam in Washington, DC.

US troop strength in Vietnam reduced to 475,000.

1970   US ground forces pull out from Cambodia.

Students killed at Kent State University and Jackson State College by National Guard troops and police.

US troop strength at 334,000.

1971   Lieutenant Calley is convicted of murder in the My Lai massacre.
        New York Times begins publication of the Pentagon Papers.
        500,000 protest the war in Washington, DC.
        US troop strength at 140,000.
1972   East Wind, an Asian American organization, founded.
        Nixon reelected President.
1973   Last US troops depart from Vietnam.
        Watergate scandal in Washington, DC.
1974   Nixon resigns as president of the US.
1975   Vietnam reunified.
1977   President Carter offers pardons to Vietnam War draft evaders.
1982   Vietnam veterans memorial is dedicated in Washington, DC.
1994   Trade embargo on Vietnam lifted.

ACKNOWLEDGEMENTS

First and foremost a special debt of gratitude to Jon Wiener, my dissertation advisor at the University of California, Irvine, for making this book possible. His initial interest in my research and his ongoing enthusiasm as my material grew from preliminary interviews into a major project, together with his guidance and direction from the very beginning, helped to bring this project into its current form. Christian G. Appy and Roy A. Rosenzweig read the initial manuscript and made cogent remarks concerning the overall content of the material. And a special thanks to Jane Hindle at Verso for bringing this manuscript together in a timely fashion for publication.

To the students at Irvine Valley College who took my American History courses and expressed an interest in listening to my ongoing research on the Vietnam War, I wish to express my appreciation for their encouragement and interest in this project. A special thanks to the faculty and staff of Humanities and Languages at IVC—to Dan Rivas, Frank Marmolejo, Rebecca Welch, Lisa Alvarez, Andrew Tonkavitch, and Roy Bauer—where I have taught for the past three years learning the craft of teaching and the politics of the ongoing struggle for social justice within the academic institution.

My gratitude to the following vets for inviting me to their homes and making first the interviews and ultimately this book possible: Lily (Lee) Adams, Bob Asada, Yoshi Ashikaga, Jimmy Chung, Duane Ebata, John Fukasawa, Mike Hama, Robert Hasuike, Gary Hayakawa, Kenneth Hay-

ashi, Darrell Higuchi, Glen Higuchi, Victor Hughes, Tom Imai, Russell Ishii, Dennis Ishiki, Phil Imamura, Calvin Kato, Victor Kato, Ken Kitagawa, Frank Kobashi, George Koide, Albert Koizumi, Dennis Kudo, Kenji Kudo, Mark Maeda, Aki Maehara, Lance Matsushita, David Miyoshi, Takeshi Mori, Ken Mui, Michael Nagaoka, Tosh Nakano, Mike Nishida, Jimmy Ohara, Vincent Okamoto, Lipo Rosero, Howard Saiki, Ed Sakishama, Roy Sasaki, Dave Shimahara, Timothy Shur, Mas Sueda, Minoru Takimoto, Kenneth Tanaka, Jerry Teshima, Roy Tsuneta, Tadashi Tsushima, Miles Uyeda, Mike Watanabe, Mike Wong, Michael Yamamoto, "Skip" Yokoda, Craig Yonemura, Eddie Yorizane, Ron Yorizane, Lane Yoshiyama, and Steve Yusa.

Special thanks to Bernie and Angel for providing a soft sofa, good company, and chauffer service in their TransAm on my research trip to Washington, DC; Osborne, Cydney, and Kefing for their hospitality and vast video collection of *chambara* [samurai] flicks on my research trip to San Jose; Stan Hall for his continual encouragement; Rex and Shirley, and David and Hilda for engaging late-night conversations, games of triple solitaire, tall glasses of Scotch on ice, strong coffee, and excellent cream puffs on my trips to the San Francisco Bay area. Special thanks to Jerry Melnyk at the Vet Center in Los Angeles; Ken Mochizuki in Seattle, Washington; Ruth Auerbach for her initial suggestions on visiting the local veteran counseling center; our lovely neighbors Daud and Belina Perez who filled our lives with music and good company; Pedro Vargas for his splendid illustrations; Philip DeBolske for his design input; Maurice and Aleene Friedman for years of friendship and dialogue; and Sally Landworth for countless evenings of dining experience throughout the greater Los Angeles area. I could not have finished the manuscript without the assistance and help of Christi Nichols in transcribing the tapes and Margaret Ryan whose editing skills made this a readable book. Funding for this research was provided by a University of California, Irvine, Graduate Opportunity Dissertation Fellowship for the academic year 1994–95.

ACKNOWLEDGEMENTS

Lastly, I give my deepest love and gratitude to my wife Lisa and our son Kai for having lived with this project for the past three years. To James, Daniel, Zav, Noah, and Kai; may your generation be filled with peace and justice.